25 Tango Lessons

25 Tango Lessons

Some of the things tango taught me about life and vice versa

ANDREA SHEPHERD

Illustrations and cover art by Juan C. Raggo
Edited by Laura Major

First Printing, 2021

ISBN 978-1-7776975-0-1

To all those who love tango as much as I do.

CONTENTS

ACKNOWLEDGEMENTS

This project would not have been possible without the help and encouragement of the many people who contributed to its realization in direct but also indirect ways. My enormous thanks go to:

Artist Juan C. Raggo, whose work I love and who generously agreed to collaborate with me on this project, thus beautifying its pages.

My smart, talented, generous, and hardworking editors and translators, whose edits, suggestions and questions made my writing better: François Camus, Laura Major and André Valiquette.

Wonderful photographer Isabelle-Blanche Pinpin, who managed to put me at ease in front of the camera and uncover my hidden photogenic side.

My blog readers, fans, and commentators, who helped me believe that the things I write are worth reading. Marcel Vachon and everyone else who said, "You should write a book!"

All the tango teachers who contributed to my development or career as a tango dancer, including those who taught me in my early years and those with whom I have worked in more recent years, notably: Caroline Demers, Carlos Gavito, Santiago Gimenez, Leandro Haeder, Hebe Hernández, Corinne Krikorian, Jorge López, Luis López, Juliana Maggioli, Sandra Naccache, Sil-

1

vana Nuñez, Mylène Pelletier, Diane Rivest, Ivan Romero, Bobby Thompson, and Jean-Sébastien Viard.

The two dance teachers who got me started on my path: Nancy Scheiber, who taught me as a young child the essential lesson of how to walk heel to toe as well as how to express myself with my body, and Helena Voronova, my tough and beloved ballet teacher throughout my teenage years.

My yoga teachers, who have contributed enormously to my dancing, teaching, and understanding of posture and anatomy as well as of myself and my own body: Hervé Blondon, Clearlight Gerald, Joanne Gormley, Joanne Ransom, François Raoult, and (especially) Josephine Vittoria.

My students, who are too many to name, but from whom I learn as much as they learn from me.

My family members who have always believed in me and supported me in my writing and dancing endeavours: my parents, Harvey and Jean Shepherd; my children, Mia Mercado-Shepherd and Shane Shepherd; my brother and sister-in-law, Hugh Shepherd and Sandra Cohen; my lifelong best friend, Dawn Lemieux; and last, but not in any way least, my partner in life, love, dance, and business, Wolf Mercado, with whom I have grown as a dancer, a teacher, and a person for nearly two decades. You believed in us and our tango dream more than anyone, including myself, and I thank you for supporting me in every single project I have embarked on, from tango to yoga to writing and much, much more.

~ Introduction ~

LIFE IS A TANGO

It's a bit strange to be compiling essays for this collection during the COVID-19 pandemic, when social activities like tango are largely shut down. I fear for the future of the dance I love. But tango has had several declines over the last century or so, and it has always come back stronger than ever. Let's hope this time will be no exception.

Tango changed my life and in many ways became my life. I started dancing tango socially in 1997; a decade later, I left my career as a copy editor and writer to open my own tango studio and dedicate myself to it full time. It is so much more than a new career: It's a passion, a community, and a way of life. Teaching tango involves more than dance instruction. History, culture, psycho-emotional issues, and interpersonal relationships all come into play. I saw this again and again in my daily life of running a studio, and I finally felt the need to write down my thoughts and share them. So in 2014, I wrote a blog post. Then another and another. I gathered a small following and people started telling me I should write a book.

But a project like that takes time. I was busy raising my family and running my business, so it sat in the back of my mind for a few years. And then this pandemic happened. While it's been terrible for tango, it has allowed me to get back to the things I've neglected—including writing.

I don't consider myself a great authority on the history of tango, but over the past 20-something years I have become an experienced teacher and a passionate observer of human nature. Just about everything in tango is a microcosm of life at large, and just about everything we learn on the dance floor is a life lesson as well. Meanwhile, we can apply what we know about life to our dancing, from how we behave in relationships to how we move our bodies.

So life is a tango—one that has taught me a lot of lessons over the years.

I hope you enjoy your read and learn something about tango or life or both along the way.

Note to readers: I believe it is important to be sensitive and inclusive when it comes to language and gender. Tango, a traditionally male-female partner dance that is rapidly evolving, contains its own challenges and particularities. The majority of leaders are still men and the majority of women are still followers, so sometimes I refer to them that way. But I refer to leaders as "her" and followers as "him" just as often. As much as possible, I try to be gender-neutral, using pronouns like "you," "we," or "they." And then there are the widely used terms "leader" and "follower," which I employ frequently in both my writing and my teaching. These terms have their own drawbacks, which I address in some of the lessons. Additional information can be found in "Tango terminology" at the back of the book. There, you will also find definitions for most of the Spanish and tango words I use.

Find me online at:
andreashepherd.ca
montango.ca
lifeisatango.blogspot.com

~ Lesson 1 ~

TANGO EVOLVES AND
THEREFORE SO MUST WE

I took my very first tango class in 1997. In 2017, I began writing a series of 20 essays to celebrate my 20th year dancing tango. Now it's 2021, which means next year will mark a quarter century of tango for me. And what a journey it has been so far!

So has it all been worth it? Absolutely.

Has it been easy? Of course not.

I have learned to be confident and humble, to let go and to stand up for myself, to be both tougher and more understanding, to lead and to follow, to express myself and to listen, to be engaged and relaxed, to think ahead while living in the moment, to follow the rules while thinking outside the box. I have learned from 25 years of change—in myself, in my city, in tango trends and customs, and in the dance itself.

Back when I was a beginner, learning tango was all about learning the steps. By the time I'd finished Tango 2, I knew not just *ochos* and *giros* but *ganchos* and *boleos, barridas* and *sacadas*. However, teachers were not really talking about following the line of dance, or the *ronda*—beyond mentioning the fact that things move in a generally counter-clockwise direction on the dance floor. Few local DJs played *cortinas* to separate the *tandas*, or sets of songs. And nobody used the *cabeceo* (the traditional non-verbal way to select partners).

About this same time, the Broadway show *Forever Tango* was touring the world. Sally Potter's movie *The Tango Lesson* and Carlos Saura's *Tango* were just being released. All around us were flashy moves and dramatic music; Pugliese instrumentals and soundtracks echoed everywhere. A new group called Gotan Project would soon demonstrate a thoroughly modern sound—a sign of things to come. Meanwhile, tango shoes from Argentina were not yet readily available, so we all danced in whatever we could find: ballroom shoes, leather-soled street shoes, or pumps held on to our feet with elastics. Montreal was already a major player on the North American tango scene, but you could only find one *milonga* each night. Still, that was seven nights of dancing a week. The whole community knew where to go for it, so most events were a guaranteed success.

Ten years later, a couple of local studios were selling Comme il Faut and Neo Tango shoes from Argentina, and all the best *tangueras'* feet were decked out in colourful, glittery open-toed stilettos. Montreal's tango scene had begun to expand beyond the central Plateau and downtown areas, spreading east, west, and even out to an off-island suburb or two. Gotan Project's brand of electronica-tango fusion music was all the rage and being reinvented by Bajofondo, Narcotango, Tanghetto, Otros Aires, and countless others. Paradoxically, the traditional *cortina* system was now being used in most milongas, but so was a huge dose of modern and experimental tango music, from Gotan Project and other *nuevo* groups to such alternative choices as The Beatles, Tom Waits and Edith Piaf. Along with the *nuevo* music came a limits-pushing style of dance most people also called tango *nuevo*. It featured a signature elastic embrace, experimental off-axis figures, and huge *boleos* executed by flexible young *tangueras* in funky, comfy tango pants. Traffic on many dance floors was a bit of a nightmare.

Soon after came a strong backlash against *nuevo* tango music and dance styles that take up more than their share of space on the floor. In the last decade, the music of the Golden Age has made a quick and powerful comeback, along with close-embrace, line-of-dance-friendly, *milonguero*-style dancing. Now, no DJ foregoes *cortinas* and just about all teachers and high-level dancers are pushing use of the *cabeceo* and respect for the *ronda*. High-end tango shoes imported from Argentina and Europe are sold in tango studios everywhere. So are tango-specific clothes made in limited editions by small designers. Roomy pants are out and curve-hugging, knee-length skirts are in because no one is kicking up their legs anymore—at least not in the *milongas*.

Montreal is still a great tango city, but countless other cities in North America and around the world have caught on, caught up and even surpassed us. Tango has gone totally global, thanks in large part to YouTube, Facebook and other social media. The prevalence of travel has also helped: Trends in music and dancing follow the dancers, so we are influenced more and more by the style and moves of maestros from Argentina and around the world. Here in Montreal, *milongas* have been sprouting up like mushrooms in recent years, within and well past the city limits. There can be up to five tango events on offer some nights, which means there's lots of choice for dancers, but organizers are by no means ensured success.

Some long-time dancers are nostalgic for the old days, when things were supposedly simpler, friendlier, and more carefree. But I believe that in tango, as in life, people view the past through rose-coloured glasses. Maybe nobody was cutting into our fun by nagging us about the line of dance, but careless navigation was rampant and there were plenty of collisions on the dance floor. Maybe nobody was pushing us to use the awkward *cabeceo,* but there were all those awkward rejections, embarrassing refusals, and sorry excuses. Maybe it was a cinch to find your friends at that one event on Friday night, but there were fewer choices, and isn't variety the spice of life? In any case, the way it was is the way it was, and the way it is is the way it is . . . until the next evolution, which is in motion already.

What *is* next? Well, teachers are continuing to move away from complex sequences and impressive moves and toward good posture, precise musicality, strong technique, and an ideal embrace. They're also enforcing respect for the line of dance and use of the *cabeceo.* (Yay!) In terms of the music, there is a backlash against the backlash, with many dancers demanding that DJs think past the Golden Age once again. Beyond that, I can only wait and see like everybody else. And I look forward to it!

For the past year, tango has primarily been danced online and in our living rooms. More than ever we are all looking back with nostalgia and forward with anticipation. I can't wait for the return of social tango and big milongas as well as to witness how the dance will evolve following this global crisis.

~ Lesson 2 ~

THE LANGUAGE OF TANGO

When teaching tango, studying tango, or just talking about tango, we compare the dance to many things: driving, sports, cats, architecture, relationships ... But my favourite analogy is language. Though I didn't invent this idea, I use the comparison often, because, to me, it feels most true.

First, tango is inarguably a form of communication. It is a non-verbal conversation between two people. The leader initiates the conversation, the follower responds, and the leader responds to her response. As in verbal exchanges, the best communicators are excellent listeners. It is such a pleasure to lead dancers who wait for the lead, who respond to subtle movements, and who take the time and initiative to express themselves. Meanwhile, leaders who give their partners space for self-expression and time to complete a movement before suggesting the next one are a joy to dance with.

As in verbal communication, interrupting is impolite. For leaders, this would be the equivalent of not letting the follower complete one movement before leading the next. For followers, it means anticipating what comes next and not waiting for the lead. If I interrupt you when you're talking to me, I'm basically telling you that what you're saying doesn't interest me or is less interesting than what I have to say. It's the same on the dance floor.

The beauty of humanity is that we are all different, and therefore we all express ourselves differently. No two conversations are alike. In the context of tango, it's important not just to understand this but also to respect it. Every follower will respond differently to a lead, and every leader will respond differently to the follower's response. And so the conversation evolves.

Of course, a dancer's skill level has a lot to do with the extent to which they can express themselves. This takes me to the second way tango is like language: the learning process. You need to learn the alphabet before you can write poetry—in English, French, Spanish, or tango.

When we teach or learn the dance, we generally start with a few simple phrases: a box step, an eight-count basic, forward and backward *ochos* within a simple structure. It's important to learn the fundamentals correctly and not get carried away by the fancy, impressive moves (fancy, impressive words). But ultimately, dancers need to go beyond the ready-made sequences and learn to create their own. If they don't, they will merely mimic their teachers or other dancers rather than express themselves. So that's the essential learning process. We follow the rules early on so that when it comes time to break some of them and write poetry, ours will be beautiful.

For most of us, tango is not a mother tongue; it is a second language. As with any language, when, where, and how we learn tango has a lot to do with becoming fluent. We know that formal study is an important component. Again, we must comprehend the underlying rules and learn to speak correctly. Taking classes, going regularly to practices and *milongas,* and dancing with different partners will all contribute to a dancer's advancement. But if we want to master a new language, the best way is to immerse ourselves in it. Speaking the language on a regular basis with a variety of people who also speak it will help immensely. Heading to Buenos Aires for your immersion is the obvious choice, but you don't have to go to Argentina to learn Argentine tango, just as you don't have to go to Spain to learn Spanish. You simply need to be where the language is spoken—or the tango is danced—frequently and at a high level. Montreal, Paris, Istanbul, and countless other cities around the world offer enough immersion that you can learn tango to the point of mastery if you want to. But studying the history, learning about the culture, and visiting the birthplace of tango will give you another level of understanding and a deeper perspective.

Some people have a knack for tango, just as some people have a knack for language. They'll pick it up in no time. But anyone, knack or not, can learn the language of tango with hard work, study, and lots and lots of practice. Some might go on to be poets in their own right, while others will just manage to make themselves understood.

I'm often contacted by dancers of ballroom, salsa, swing, and other dances. Sometimes they expect to begin tango at an intermediate level, since they already know how to dance. But if I speak English well and I want to learn Russian, does that mean I should be put in an intermediate-level Russian class? Of course not! However, if I already speak two or three languages, there's a good chance that I'll pick up a fourth one more quickly than someone who has never learned a second language. People who dance other dances are probably coming in with a good sense of musicality, a certain amount of body awareness, and a number of other skills that may accelerate the learning process, but they still need to start at the beginning.

So we've covered how to learn the language of tango, but what does it mean to master it?

If we've learned to walk with a partner in front of us, we're already communicating at a basic level—but we need a certain amount of vocabulary and a certain ease of expression to really say we dance tango. At the same time, big, impressive words do not a great communicator make. Instead of trying to impress our partners with vocabulary that goes right over their heads, use words (moves) that they can understand and follow. We may know the big words, but it's important to use them in the right context and with the right people. This is how we can be good communicators, which is key to tango mastery.

What else is key? Excellent listening skills, a desire and an ability to express yourself, strong basics, a thorough understanding of the rules and also when to break them, a well-developed yet carefully chosen vocabulary, an awareness of and respect for your partner's abilities . . . The list is long. Mastering this language goes far beyond knowing its mechanics. Yes, we need to know the rules and the structure, but we must also be able to express ourselves with fluidity and eloquence. We need to go beyond the language itself and develop our communication skills and our creativity. Finally, we need to remember that no matter how well we ourselves may speak (or think we speak) the language of tango, we are still learning. No one knows all the words in the dictionary. Besides, languages evolve and so should we.

A note to the advanced tango speakers: You can help newcomers learn our language. How? By leaving the lessons to the teachers and the class setting. Imagine if you were having a conversation with someone, telling them about something really interesting that happened to you. Now, imagine that the person you were talking to stopped you every few words to correct your pronunciation, suggest a different idiom, tell you a better way to phrase your thoughts. Perhaps you would learn something from these instructions, but it wouldn't be a very enjoyable conversation. All you need to do to help beginners move forward is speak (dance) slowly and clearly to make sure they can understand you. They will learn from you and have fun doing it.

~ Lesson 3 ~

NO TEACHING ON THE DANCE FLOOR

Teaching on the dance floor is my Number One pet peeve—and I say this as a teacher, a *milonga* organizer, and a dancer.

Being taught or corrected by our dance partners makes us feel bad. This is true for leaders and followers alike. First, it interrupts the flow of conversation that is the dance, leaving little chance we'll experience the wonderful feeling that comes after a particularly connected *tanda*. Second, it puts the "instructor" in a position of authority or superiority, deserved or not (let's assume not). Consequently, the instructee feels inferior, and this imbalance destroys the idea of an equal partnership. Third, the act of instructing our partners immediately assigns blame for any miscommunication, inviting feelings of defensiveness or inadequacy. These negative feelings may be fleeting, but sometimes they can linger, putting a damper on the whole evening or even the entire tango experience.

The blame game

As a teacher, I disapprove of self-appointed dance-floor instructors for many reasons, not the least of which is that they undermine the work that real teachers do. We have training and experience and expertise. We have a method that we have spent years developing. We have technique as dancers and as teachers—and we understand both roles. Different teachers will have different levels of mastery of the "other" role, but any decent teacher will have developed at least a solid competency in both. This allows us to understand both sides of a situation when a "mistake" is made. Any experienced dancer may be able to see what the mistake itself is, but it is unlikely anyone but a teacher will be able to figure out the underlying reason for it. We can then figure out a solution that ideally does not assign blame but instead involves a tweak or improvement on both sides.

Let's say a couple is dancing and the follower loses her alignment (and therefore her balance) whenever she pivots a certain way. Her leader may notice that her "mistake" is her lopsided posture at the moment of pivot. Thinking he has the solution, he might tell her not to lean over or not to push on his hand. But that leader might not realize that he is in fact throwing her off balance—he is changing the position of his arm, abruptly shifting her points of reference and making it difficult for her to stay straight. A follower in this same situation might blame her leader for throwing off her pivots. However, there are many adjustments she herself could make to stay straight and balanced regardless of her leader's technical shortcomings: keeping both feet on the floor, pointing her toes slightly outward, and not allowing her pelvis to swing forward.

In our classes, my partner and I actively discourage instruction and correction among students even during class time. It is the behaviour we receive the most complaints about—from singles who want to switch partners (or drop out altogether) and from couples whose uncomfortable conflicts on the floor might follow them home after class. (My teaching partner and I feel that the work we do is in part couples therapy.)

Outside of class, the rules of etiquette apply to teachers, too. In fact, we should set the example. When we are dancing, we are not teachers—we are dancers. We teach those who come to us for lessons, but just because we *can* teach doesn't mean we should make it our mission to offer unsolicited advice or modify the style or technique of every dancer we touch. Anyway, we deserve to take off our teacher hats and just relax and enjoy the dance in our off hours!

Don't block the flow

As a *milonga* organizer, I dislike impromptu lessons because they block the flow of a *milonga* both on and off the floor. Tango is a social dance, which means we are not only dancing with our partners—we are also dancing with all the other couples on the floor. The best dance-floor flow happens when all the dancers are paying attention to what's going on around them while trying to keep things moving forward. The couple who is standing on the spot teaching, discussing, or trying to figure out a move is creating a bottleneck behind them and thus blocking the dance-floor flow.

So that covers flow on the floor, but how does this behaviour break the flow off the floor?

I can't count how many people have complained to me over the years about "teachy" partners and their condescending comments. I've seen people leave angry or in tears after a particularly unpleasant *tanda* because the flow or enjoyment of their evening was ruined by one insensitive partner. If one dancer has a negative experience at my *milonga*, the flow of the evening as a whole is affected. The occasional bad experience is impossible to avoid, but there is one way every dancer can contribute positively: Don't teach on the dance floor!

Negative feelings

As a dancer, I despise being taught, corrected, or commented on while I'm dancing; it eliminates that state of abandon I so enjoy when there is a good connection. It also brings up unpleasant feelings like disappointment, self-doubt, defensiveness, and resentment. Sarcastic responses play around in my head—but I'm polite and a professional, so they don't come out of my mouth. I grin and bear the rest of the dance and do my best to avoid that particular dancer in the future.

And I'm lucky. I do most of my dancing at my own *milongas*, so even the worst offenders don't try to teach me. But I do get the occasional condescending "muy bien" (which is well-intentioned I'm sure but feels like a pat on the head). I also sometimes get an explainer: If a *tanguero* tries to lead a particularly complex sequence of fancy moves and I miss something, he will try to explain what I "should have" done. Inside, I'm screaming, "*Should have?* Really? Well, you *should have* led it properly if that's what you wanted me to do. And by the way, try just walking a couple of steps now and then. Listen to the music and give the unending cycle of *ganchos* and *volcadas* a rest." But outside, I just smile and nod.

I was floored when a fellow teacher told me about an experience she had. She's a young and very talented tango dancer at the beginning of what promises to be a long career. A man we both know—a decent social dancer who rubs people the wrong way with some of his judgmental and condescending remarks—informed her that she had become a pretty good dancer. He said he would rate her a 7. As in out of 10.

I've shown examples of bad leader behaviour here because I'm a woman and most often a follower, so that is my experience. But followers can be just as guilty of offering unwelcome advice on how to embrace, walk, and lead. Leaders have plenty of stories to tell about followers who offer such helpful little comments as, "It shows that you don't really practise often." Unbelievable!

It's no wonder we feel self-doubt when faced with situations like these. But next time you find yourself with a "teachy" dance partner, remember that dancers who regularly correct their partners are not among the most skilled on the floor. Leaders who correct frequently are probably attempting moves that either they or their partners are not ready for. Followers who correct frequently have underdeveloped following skills. (Good followers can follow just about any lead, regardless of level.) Those who correct their partners do so because they don't know how to correct themselves.

Don't get me wrong, we all could improve our dancing—amateurs and professionals alike. As a teacher, I need to work harder than anyone on my technique so I can set the best example possible. But there's a time and a place to teach and be taught, and the *milonga* isn't it.

As dancers, it is not up to us to mould our partners into the dancers we would like them to be. We should accept them as the dancers they are and adapt ourselves to them for the 10 minutes a *tanda* lasts. If we all tried to adapt ourselves, we would come much closer to finding that 50/50 balance that makes a dance feel just right.

Instead of looking for what needs to be fixed in the dancers we dance with, let's find something positive in each one. Maybe he has a perfect sense of rhythm; maybe she conveys true passion. How about we all just relax and enjoy things a little more, leave the lessons for the classes, and keep our judgments (or scores!) to ourselves. And, as I tell my kids, if we can't say anything nice, we're better off saying nothing at all. (Well, we do have to say "thank you.")

~ Lesson 4 ~

THE FIVE ESSENTIAL CONNECTIONS

Dancing tango is all about connection. We must connect to our partners, of course, but it doesn't end there. Establishing a thorough connection with the following five entities will help us dance tango to our fullest potential and enjoyment.

Connection one: the partner

This is the most obvious and indisputable connection. The old cliché "It takes two to tango" exists for a reason. Tango is the quintessential couple dance. Without a partner, there is no tango.

However, this does not mean we need a *regular* partner. In tango, we aim to find, create, and build an intense connection in a very short time. It is part of the beauty, the allure, and the challenge of tango. This can be done with one regular partner or with a variety of rotating ones. Or both. Maybe tonight we will dance only with each other, but tomorrow night we will dance with half the dancers in the room. It doesn't matter. During each dance, everything we do should be caused or inspired by the person we are dancing with.

If we can focus more on our partners than on ourselves, we will shine in our role—whether we are leader or follower. If we help our partners by leading or following better, by waiting for and being patient with them, we will allow them to dance with more ease and enjoyment. In turn, *we* will dance with more ease and enjoyment. The tango relationship is not linear; it is circular. It is a constant give-and-take between the two partners, so whatever we give, we will get back. Which brings us to the second essential connection.

Connection two: the self

If it's all about our partners, why do we need a deep connection with ourselves? Well, because it's not *all* about our partners. It's about the couple, and we are 50 percent of the couple. They say you can't really love someone else if you don't love yourself first. Well, you also can't really know someone else if you don't know yourself first.

For tango teachers, lack of body awareness is one of the hardest obstacles to overcome when working with a student. Many people come to tango in middle age, and it's often the case that they have never taken a dance class in their lives. Such students have limited body awareness when they start out. Perhaps they've never paid attention to—let alone tried to control—the counter-movements that occur in their bodies when they move. Maybe they've never thought about the position of their hips in relation to their feet and shoulders. It's possible they've never tried to simultaneously drop their shoulders and raise their hearts while keeping their knees soft and their arms relaxed but in contact with another person. It's a lot for anyone to think about at once, but it's especially overwhelming for someone to whom these concepts are entirely new. This doesn't mean that someone who has never danced can't learn tango at age 50 or 60. Absolutely they can, and many do. But body awareness is one more aspect of learning that takes hard work, practice, and patience. (Disciplines such as yoga and Pilates are wonderful for building body awareness—as well as strength, flexibility, and balance—and are excellent supplements to tango lessons.)

If we know our bodies and ourselves, we will have better balance and overall control of our own movements. We will also be more inclined to trust ourselves to lead what we intend or follow what we feel. We need to know ourselves as deeply as we know our partners. So it's not *all* about our partners; it's about ourselves and our partners. If we know both and care for both, we will be on our way to dancing as one, which is what we strive for. We could in fact roll these first two connections into one entity: the couple, made up of two separate but equal parts. But while we should strive to move and breathe as one, we both bring ourselves to the dance. We must not be so passive that we lose our own identities, and we must not be so dominant that we overshadow our partner.

Connection three: the music

This connection is my personal favourite. Music is literally what moves me. It is the inspiration behind my every step and every gesture.

But musicality is a funny thing in Argentine tango. We can improvise so widely on the music, and there are no set patterns forcing us to start something new with each new phrase or mark every strong beat with metronome-like regularity. Because of this, teachers often avoid setting sequences to music in any specific way—and students often ignore the music completely. They say that it's too much to think about on top of everything else. But this is a mistake. The dance and the music cannot be treated as separate entities. If students get used to treating the music as background noise, it will be difficult to backtrack later and use the rhythm as the driving force that guides their every action.

As dancers, we should be living and breathing the music, marking the rhythm and painting the melody. Otherwise, why choose tango music or indeed any music at all? We dance differently to every type of music and to every orchestra—or at least we should. It's not enough to just listen to and follow the music: We need to let the music into our bodies and our hearts, let it lead us, let it become one with us. Just like that perfect partner.

Connection four: the floor

This one sounds obvious, yet it's amazing how many people have trouble keeping both feet on the floor. Sure, we all know we must touch the floor when we walk; gravity doesn't give us much of a choice. But it's more than that in tango. We need to be fully aware of the ground and our connection to it. The ground, well, grounds us. It supports us, stabilizes us, and gives us power.

The ground supports us best when we work *with* gravity, letting it soften our knees and weigh down our feet, hips, and shoulders. Then we can stand straight and tall, lengthening the spine and lifting the heart for both balance and elegance. In yoga, when we do a tree pose, we talk about the roots—a tree's connection to the ground—being what allows it to stand so tall and not fall over. It is the same for a tango dancer.

The floor stabilizes us when we have both feet in connection with it as often as possible. The supporting leg grounds our axis and the free leg widens our base of support, providing an anchor. Think of how a tree's roots spread out beyond the base of its trunk.

The floor gives us power when we use our supporting leg to propel our movements—both steps and pivots. This power provides ease of movement and a clear message to our partners.

Teachers talk about caressing the floor, licking the floor (with our feet, of course!), painting on the floor, being friends with the floor, and knowing the floor intimately, including every crack, bulge, and dent. Do all of these things. Be one with the floor and it will help you be one with yourself, your partner, and the music.

Connection five: those around us

The last connection is by no means the least important. Many dancers neglect this one, though.

We often say that when things are just right with our partner, the rest of the world disappears. It's like we're dancing in a bubble. While this is true, our bubble must be transparent so that we don't collide with or entirely pop other couples' bubbles mid-*tanda*. We need to dance respectfully. We should limit backward steps, refrain from tailgating, avoid abruptly cutting in front of others, and ensure we are not taking up too much space on a crowded floor.

But instead of just dancing *around* all the other couples and treating them like obstacles, we should try to dance *with* them. If everyone did this, the flow in the *milongas* would be fluid, pleasant, and easy to navigate. When we dance tango socially, as most of us do, all those other dancers are an integral part of our art and our experience. We need to accept that and accept that our dancing plans and patterns will constantly change and evolve because of what's happening around us. Not easy, perhaps, but imagine the payoff: the whole room moving as one to the same music on the same floor, each body different, each partner different, but everything in harmony. It would be tango bliss.

Every now and then, all five connections will fall into place at once. Our bodies will move with ease and confidence, melding at once with our partners and the music, fully connected to and supported by the floor and in harmony with those around us for that perfect dance that transports us and reminds us why we so love tango.

~ Lesson 5 ~

THESE EIGHT TRAITS WILL
MAKE YOU A BETTER DANCER

There are certain physical abilities that contribute to the
ease with which we learn and dance tango (or any other dance

for that matter): strength, agility, balance, coordination, body awareness, good posture, and a sense of rhythm, to name a few.

But it takes more than superb poise and impressive footwork to become the tango dancer everyone lines up for. It takes partnering skills, which have as much to do with who you are as what you can do.

Here are eight personality traits that will help you on your way to becoming not just the ultimate dancer but also the ultimate partner.

Patience

We all know that patience is a virtue—and the old cliché holds true on the dance floor. We have to be patient with ourselves when learning and when dancing. Argentine tango is challenging and takes a lot of focus and a lot of practice. I'm the first to assert that anyone can learn it, but we all learn differently and at different speeds. Impatience—and the frustration that comes with it—is often the deal-breaker for students.

Of course, it doesn't help if our partners are impatient with us. We must remember to extend our patience to ourselves *and* to others. It's too easy to blame our partner for the "mistakes" we make when dancing with them. But before we sigh, roll our eyes, or make that passive-aggressive little comment, we need to remember something: *We* may be dancing with someone who still has some learning to do, but so is *our partner*. And this is true for all of us, forever. Sure, we know more after 10 years than 10 weeks, but we are never done learning and improving our own skills.

Patience involves letting go of our plans and going with the flow, forgiving ourselves and our partners for those "mistakes" that really aren't mistakes at all—just perfectly normal moments of miscommunication that can easily become opportunities for evolution and creativity. Patience also makes it easier for us to wait for the music, to take pleasure from it, and to go with the flow on the dance floor. This is infinitely better than speeding around, weaving in and out of our lane and cutting off other dancers.

Trust

This can be a tough one, but it's also a huge one. If we are to find that true tango connection, we must trust our partners.

For a leader, this means trusting that our partner is capable not just of following us but also of *dancing*. Trusting in these two things means we will lead with confidence rather than hesitation, being clear while leaving it to the follower to stay with us and the music. Also, if we trust our partner to dance, we will avoid the common mistake of over-leading. Remember, a leader's job is not to *take* their partner from Point A to Point B; it is to *invite* and then *allow* their partner to take that step.

For a follower, this means trusting our partner to lead *something*. If I don't trust my leader, I will do what I *think* they meant to lead rather than what they actually led. I don't need to know what my leader was thinking—I only need to know what my leader did.

So we have to trust the other, but it is equally important that we trust ourselves.

If leaders don't trust themselves, they will hesitate—and then so will their partners.

If followers don't trust themselves, they will do what they think rather than what they feel. Too many followers second-guess themselves constantly. "Was that right?" "What was that move we just did?" "What's next?" All pointless questions by the time they come to mind. Once a step has been taken, it is done and can't be taken back. Right or wrong, intended or not, there is no point in judging it. All either partner can do is move on, and that is how tango is supposed to be. If we can trust *that,* we can worry less and dance more.

Self-confidence

Having self-confidence is similar to trusting ourselves. This quality will help us lead or follow with ease and clarity and without hesitation or second-guesses. It's not an easy trait to come by for everyone, however; it may take time and effort.

Hopefully, our partners will be patient with us, and we in turn will be patient with others. This will help build everyone's self-confidence. Practice and hard work will bring increased mastery of the dance, which should lead to more self-confidence. Once we know what we're doing, our confidence will come across to our partners and help them trust us. We don't need loads of vocabulary or years of training to be able to lead or follow; it is possible and helpful to be confident in the few things we do know. Self-confident dancers usually attract more partners, which leads to improved skills and more confidence, which leads to more partners, and so on.

But beware the fine line between self-confidence and arrogance. A healthy trust in ourselves shouldn't mean we think we're beyond fault or better than everyone else.

A sense of humour

To improve our tango dancing, we need to take it seriously—but let's not take *ourselves* too seriously.

Almost every dancer is guilty of the occasional impatient sigh directed at our partners or ourselves, or of too many words of apology when "mistakes" are made. Some dancers are guilty of pointing out every failed move and explaining what the result "should have" been. These things can stick with people, ruining a dance or a whole evening.

Here's the thing: Tango is an improvised dance. It does not always go according to plan and it *should* not always go according to plan.

Because mistakes are often not really mistakes, they usually don't need to be acknowledged. But even when a miscommunication is blatant and downright awkward, it's tango—we're supposedly in it for fun, so why not just laugh it off? Smile, forgive your partner, forgive yourself. Then everyone can relax and move on.

Passion

It is tango, after all. It's unusual for someone to be lukewarm about tango yet stick with it long enough to master it.

Tango is widely accepted to be the most complex of the couple dances because of its closeness, unique embrace, and improvised nature. This means we need to dedicate a significant amount of time (and money) to dancing if we're going to get anywhere approaching an advanced level. Once a week is not enough: We must go to class, we must practise, we must dance in the *milongas*. Six months of experience is nothing. So we'd better be pretty passionate about it. That passion will keep us going and elevate our dancing beyond solid technique and a good sense of rhythm. People will see this and, of course, our partners will feel it.

Generosity

Skilled dancers tend to be in demand, for obvious reasons. Young, attractive dancers tend to be in demand, too. But there's another kind of dancer people keep coming back to: fun dancers. If I dance with you and enjoy myself, I will surely seek you out again—and I will spread the word.

Skill level, musicality, and many other attributes can make a dancer fun, but the most enjoyable dancers are those who put their partners first. By dancing to your partner's level, you make them feel confident; by not using your partner as a shield or battering ram on the dance floor, you make them feel respected; by laughing off any blips, you make them feel at ease and in the moment. Tango dancers with a generous spirit put their partners' enjoyment and wellbeing before their own, and it comes back to them in the end: A dancer with happy partners is inevitably a happy dancer.

Good listening skills

In life and in tango, the best communicators are good listeners.

Followers are told from the start that they need to follow, or listen to, their partners. Later on, followers learn that their role is about much more than following: They also need to express themselves in the dance. That's when the real fun begins. Those who learn in that order—listen first and then talk—become the best at what they do. Those who "talk" too much and listen too little tend to guess and anticipate. They lack that connection that would otherwise make them a pleasure to dance with.

Leaders are taught to *lead*, but they often don't realize they also need to follow. The leader invites his partner to take a step, allows her to take that step, and then follows her through it. In other words, he allows her to speak and listens to what she has to say. This way, the leader ensures he allows his partner to complete a movement before he indicates something new. Those leaders who drag their partners around, making them feel like it's all they can do to keep up? They are the ones who aren't listening. Attentive leaders are the ones who allow their partners to express themselves, to decorate the dance, to contribute to the musicality. They are the ones who are the most fun and rewarding to dance with, for beginners and advanced dancers alike.

Presence

Physical presence is essential for tango dancers. A passive leader is hard to follow, while a passive follower is boring. Dancers often talk about the "resistance" or the "pressure" that one should feel from one's partner. I dislike both words because they imply that we should somehow block our partners or push them away. For me, the correct word here is "presence," which accurately implies that we should be strong in our dancing while looking for that meeting and exchange of energy with the other.

But there is another type of presence that is helpful for tango dancers: the ability to live fully and completely in the moment. If we're guessing what comes next, working our way toward the next impressive move, or judging ourselves or our partners, we are not truly present. As a result, our connection will be lacking. One of the things I love most about dancing tango is that I can abandon myself to the dance, no matter what happened before or what might come later. I would go so far as to say (and I'm not the first to say it) that I enter a meditative state when I'm dancing Argentine tango. Those who have a knack for living in the moment may take quite easily to tango, while those who don't may find that tango helps them to let go a little.

If you already possess any of the above-mentioned qualities, certain aspects of tango will come naturally to you. But the great thing is that tango can also aid you in developing those traits that may not come so naturally. This won't just help you in tango; it will help you in life.

After all, life is a tango, is it not?

~ Lesson 6 ~

IT'S NICE TO BE IMPORTANT, BUT IT'S MORE IMPORTANT TO BE NICE

I've sometimes thought that the tango community would do well to take the above saying to heart.

I remember a social media post by a local dancer that sparked ongoing and heated discussion. In the post, the dancer criticized organizers and dancers (particularly male dancers) for not being more open to dancing with newcomers. He was referring especially to tourists who perhaps didn't receive as warm a welcome as they could have at a particular *milonga*, but the discussion quickly expanded. After covering the issue of newcomers to specific *milongas*, talk turned to the issue of those who feel like outsiders because they're not part of the "elite" of a given *milonga* or community. This was not the first time this particular dancer had chastised others for being overly exclusive in their invitations.

Many dancers responded to support or echo his viewpoint, but others pointed out that tango is a social activity we do for our enjoyment, and we therefore should not be "forced" to suffer through dances with people we don't enjoy dancing with. I agree that if a dance or dancer is truly insufferable, we have every reason and every right to stay away. But does each experience with someone who is just average, who is below our level, who is new to the game qualify as "suffering"? Some of the comments just sounded so self-centred and self-important. Yes, we dance tango to have fun and enjoy ourselves—but it is a social activity that takes place within a community, and while we are dancing there are two of us. So isn't other people's enjoyment, pleasure, and satisfaction as important as our own?

"It's nice to be important, but it's more important to be nice." This quote is most often attributed to U.S. businessman and billionaire John Templeton, one of the most generous philanthropists in history. As I mentioned in the previous lesson, I think many of us could benefit from injecting our tango-going selves with a little more generosity. But before any assumptions are made, allow me to point out that lack of generosity is not only a male problem. It may feel that way to the women who sit all night waiting to be invited, and it certainly can look that way in *milongas* where women outnumber men (which is often the case), but women can be just as selective, just as exclusive, just as self-centred or egotistical.

One time, my partner and I were giving a free mini lesson to beginners during an outdoor *milonga* we organize every summer. There were a few young guys who wanted to participate, but they didn't have partners. My partner went to ask a woman we both know whether she would help out for a few minutes by dancing with one of the beginners. Her reply? "Never!" I'm not sure whether that meant "I would never help you out" or "I would never help out a beginner," but either way, why would you "never" be willing to encourage a new dancer? Perhaps I shouldn't have been surprised. After a couple of years of classes, this same woman had announced that she didn't need lessons anymore. Thinking (quite mistakenly) that she had learned all she needed to, she was apparently uninterested in contributing to anyone else's education. This is simply an extreme example of an all-too-prevalent attitude.

Another woman who frequents our *milongas* once rolled her eyes at me after refusing a dance. "Why should I force myself?" she said. I just smiled politely. I guess she realized how she sounded, because she immediately tried to justify herself. "I mean, you have to force yourself because you're a teacher, but I don't have to do that.

I was unimpressed by her attitude, but I admit she made me think. Do I sometimes force myself to dance with a student because it's in my professional interest to keep them happy? Yes, I guess I do. But I'm a teacher and a human, not just a business person. I want to keep students happy because I want them to practise and to feel encouraged. I care about how other people feel and whether they succeed.

The idea that we shouldn't have to "waste our time" dancing with someone who is "below our level" feels wrong to me in more ways than one. First, we can improve our skills and, yes, even have some fun with someone who is "below our level." Second, is it really a waste of time to contribute to either the enjoyment or the improvement of others? And third, maybe our "level" isn't as high as we have led ourselves to believe. If it's that hard to dance with someone mediocre, is that more a reflection on their skills or our own?

In some tango communities, people won't dance with newcomers until they've seen them dance with someone else. You know, to make sure they're good enough. After all, we wouldn't want a "good," "cool," or "in" dancer to see us dancing with someone beneath us—that might tarnish our reputation. This attitude just reeks of snobbishness and self-importance. Is it really more crucial to look good than to help a newcomer feel welcome? And what's wrong with a little risk-taking now and then? I take risks by accepting dancers I haven't studied previously. Sometimes I endure an uncomfortable 12 minutes. But I have also had some lovely surprises and discovered some wonderful new connections.

As mentioned in the previous lesson, generosity is one of the essential qualities in a good dancer, male or female, leader or follower. Those with a generous spirit put their partners' enjoyment and well-being before their own, which ultimately ups their skills while keeping their partners happy and coming back for more.

If you really are that much better than somebody else (please keep that ego in check when self-assessing), then why not offer that person the pleasure and benefit of your experience for a few minutes? Again, I'm not saying we should force ourselves to dance with someone we find difficult or generally disagreeable, but an occasional dance with somebody new or less skilled could have far-reaching benefits. It may inspire that person to stick with tango or to work harder on improving their dancing. By sharing our time, we'll have contributed to the enjoyment and abilities of that individual dancer *and* we'll have helped grow the tango community.

We can get a lot out of helping someone else. And we get very little out of being egotistical. Egotism blocks our capacity to learn, while generosity goes hand in hand with open-mindedness. These positive qualities allow us to welcome learning, growth, and improvement of ourselves and our partners, ultimately enhancing our own enjoyment.

~ Lesson 7 ~

EMBRACE IS EVERYTHING

The first thing we feel when we meet on the floor for a *tanda* is the embrace, or *abrazo*. In those first seconds when we hold and are held by a partner, we discover a lot about that person as a dancer (and as a human, but that's a topic for another lesson). We learn whether they're confident or insecure, controlling or caring, intense or reserved, out to impress or to connect. We can sense the overall skill level of a partner right away, in those first fleeting moments, before we even take a step.

The embrace in tango is basically synonymous with the connection, and we already know that tango is all about good connection. It is through the embrace that we feel everything, so it is what allows us to lead or to be led.

Abrazo literally means embrace or hug. So our *abrazo* should contain all the elements of a good hug. It should wrap around our partners and hold them securely without being overly imposing, restrictive, or otherwise uncomfortable, and it should feel sincere.

If the embrace is all wrong—if it's pushing, pulling, blocking, being overly tense or completely lax—it doesn't matter how many cool figures or fancy embellishments you can come up with: Nothing will feel very good to your partner. If your embrace is just right, however, you won't have to do much to feel great to dance with.

On a technical level, this is how I use my own embrace and how I explain it to my students:

- Use your hands more and your arms less.
- Keep your arms soft and light and your joints—wrists, elbows, and shoulders—mobile.
- Use your hands—especially your palms—to actively hold your partner so that you feel him or her. Your hands should go beyond the surface of the clothes or even the skin and mould themselves to the body part they are in contact with.

- Keep your back active, too. The upper back muscles are what will bring your shoulders and shoulder blades down, allowing your arms to relax without being limp. This technique will also help give you an adaptable embrace. Tango is very much about adaptability, and our embrace needs to adjust to each partner and each move; if our arms are soft and our joints are mobile to begin with, the embrace will adapt effortlessly, all on its own.
- Give equal energy to both hands. Because of the asymmetrical nature of the tango embrace, this is not necessarily easy. But balancing the presence of the two hands can be an almost miraculous solution to too much push or pull on either side.

A lot of teachers say: "Keep your frame." I used to say it, too. I don't anymore, because I think it gives the wrong idea. First, in an effort to keep our frame, we will have a tendency to be too stiff. Second, the specific form of the embrace is less important than the way it functions. That's why we should be able to dance in a practice embrace, close embrace, open embrace, or even with one arm or no arms at all. If we get stuck on the exact form—the angle of the elbows, how high to hold the arms, the precise spot to place our hand on our partner's back—we become too focused on ourselves and our form. As a result, we ultimately block some of the messages we're trying to send or receive. Instead, we must hold our partner with strong hands and soft arms, discovering just the right balance between firm and supple, receptive and communicative. We must use our *abrazo* to *be* with our partner and to feel him or her—not to hold ourselves up, to control or restrict, to push or pull. "Keep your partner's frame" is a better way to put it. That way, you'll use your embrace to take care of your partner, allowing mobility while giving them consistent and helpful points of reference. This in turn will enable them to keep their axis and balance, to lead or follow you with ease, and, most importantly, to feel good.

The embrace just might be the most important element in our dancing.

Then again, posture is really important as well.

~ Lesson 8 ~

POSTURE IS EVERYTHING

I admit it: I'm pretty obsessed with good posture. Being a dance teacher and a yoga teacher, I adjust posture (mine and others'), observe posture, study posture, and think about posture every day.

You don't have to be as preoccupied with posture as I am, but let's face it—if your posture is bad, your embrace will suffer. And if your embrace is bad, your connection will be lacking. And without good connection, what is tango?

Why can't we have a good embrace without good posture? Well, just as the arms are connected to the rest of our body, the embrace is connected to the way we hold ourselves. And though "embrace" makes us think specifically of the arms and hands, we really embrace our partners with our whole bodies: hands, arms, shoulders, back, chest, head ... Even the position of the hips, legs, and feet contributes to the way we hold our partners. If your head is too far forward, for example, it might push against your partner's head in an uncomfortable way. This could hurt their neck or throw off their balance, affecting the way they hold you. If your upper back is too rounded and your shoulders are forward, your chest will cave in. This can make your partner feel that you're holding back or pushing them away rather than inviting them in.

Good posture is a huge part of good overall technique, and it frees us to dance with ease and to hold our partners comfortably. So what is good posture?

Posture refers to the position in which you hold your body upright. Good posture involves training your body to stand, walk, sit, lie, and dance in positions where the least strain is placed on supporting muscles and ligaments during movement or weight-bearing activities.

Posture and alignment go hand in hand—and correct alignment is essential for maintaining good posture. So let's look at what constitutes correct, or healthy, alignment.

Alignment refers to how the head, shoulders, spine, hips, knees, and ankles relate to and line up with each other. When dance teachers talk about "axis" and "keeping your axis," they're really talking about keeping correct alignment. Proper alignment of the body helps you achieve and maintain good posture. This is great for tango dancing and for life in general, as it means putting less stress on the spine.

There are four main points that should be aligned when we are standing:

- The lateral malleolus, or the little bone on the outside of the ankle.
- The greater trochanter, or the top part of the femur (thigh bone), located at the hip joint.
- The acromion, or the little bone at the top of the shoulder.
- The auditory meatus, or earhole.

Aligning these points maintains the natural curves of the spine, which form an "S" shape. Viewed from the side, the cervical (upper) and lumbar (lower) regions of the spine have a lordotic curve, meaning they curve inward; the thoracic (mid) region of the spine has a kyphotic curve, meaning it curves gently outward. The spine's curves work like a coiled spring to absorb shock, maintain balance, and facilitate range of motion.

In tango, as in life, correct posture and alignment can be difficult to maintain, especially if this is all new to us. Let's look at a few common issues.

Tucking the tail bone. This results in relaxing the lower back muscles, flattening the lumbar curve, and sending the centre of gravity toward the toes rather than keeping it over the heel bone (which is the largest bone in the foot and therefore made to support us). Tucking the pelvis puts strain on the feet, knees, and spine. This is particularly problematic in tango because it means your hips, legs, and feet sit farther forward than your upper body, so you will tend to bump knees with your partners, step on their toes, or get your own toes stepped on. It also results in a reduced ability to release the free leg behind you, affecting everything from your walk to your *boleos*.

"Swayback" posture. With this common postural issue, the lumbar curve is amplified and the belly (and sometimes chest) project forward in an exaggerated way. This can result in the centre of gravity being too far forward, putting pressure on the metatarsal joints and the lower back.

Holding the head too far forward. Many people either jut the chin (which compresses the cervical spine) or hang the head forward in a downward-looking position. The latter is especially prevalent in tango. What you want to do instead is keep the head back by keeping the chin parallel to the floor and sitting the skull back on top of the spine. This elongates the cervical spine while keeping its natural curve.

The good news is that when we practise good posture and alignment regularly, we gradually strengthen the necessary muscles while developing new, healthy habits. One day we realize that we're standing and sitting correctly most of the time—and it even feels natural!

A big part of the challenge (once we have found correct alignment) is to keep those points of alignment while we are in motion. What can I say except that practice makes perfect? Posture and alignment are not things to be practised an hour or two a week in tango class. They need to be practised as often as possible during your daily activities: sitting at your desk, walking down the street, waiting for the bus, brushing your teeth, and, of course, dancing.

In tango, we have the added challenge of maintaining our own alignment while moving and holding someone else. I always tell my tango students not to sacrifice their posture for anything or anyone. This means we don't contort ourselves to execute an awkwardly placed *gancho* and we don't dance hunched over because we're taller than our partner. We also don't lean forward to retain a close embrace; if I or my partner can't execute a move in close embrace while standing up straight, I should either open the embrace or forgo the move rather than sacrifice my posture.

On the subject of close embrace, there are slight sacrifices in alignment to be made when dancing in a close, *milonguero*-style *abrazo*. But when I say slight, I mean it. Because we're looking for physical connection between our own torso and that of our partner, our rib cage may sit a tiny bit forward in relation to the pelvis. However, if we keep our hips over our heels and avoid thrusting our head forward, the adjustment in our upper body will be minimal. We will be able to reach our partner, and our alignment should readjust itself automatically as soon as we release the close embrace. If the leader keeps his hips back over his heels, he should not have to lean forward at all to achieve close embrace. It is up to the follower to reach forward and find the connection with her partner. But again, if her lower body is correctly positioned, there will be little reaching necessary. Also, any forward reach should be accompanied by an upward stretch in the torso, which will lengthen the spine and prevent us from leaning in an uncomfortable or unhealthy way.

Of course, all this work on posture and alignment will help to carry us through life with less pain, fewer back problems, and better overall health. So improving our posture and alignment for tango will have benefits that reach far beyond the dance floor.

Posture might just be the most important element in our dancing.

Then again, musicality is super important, too.

~ Lesson 9 ~

MUSICALITY IS EVERYTHING

Musicality just may be my favourite subject. It's certainly my favourite quality in a dancer—well, perhaps tied for first place with a good embrace. Give me a nice embrace and a great connection to the music and I am a happy dancer.

If only I could make beginners believe this from the start: Big, impressive moves do not a great dancer make. Musicality, on the other hand . . .

For beginner and intermediate dancers, musicality is probably the most underestimated aspect of tango. From Day One, just about every leader wants to learn steps, steps, steps and moves, moves, moves. While cool and complex steps can be fun, they're nothing without a connection to the music. Better to execute something simple in perfect time to the rhythm than something seemingly complex while treating the music as mere background noise.

I think the same phenomenon exists in every social dance. A while ago I went out to a salsa club for the first time in over a decade, and I found that dancers are more focused on *moves* than ever. People were turning this way and that, executing series after series of complex figures, rarely if ever pausing to just *dance*—to just feel the music and move to it. In tango, as in salsa, complex sequences and difficult moves can be fun and satisfying when expertly executed, but there needs to be some simple dancing in between. And if the execution is not expert, if either partner is off the music, it's disconcerting to the other and, frankly, barely any fun at all. For the follower, it means you're constantly receiving two conflicting messages—one from your partner and one from the soundtrack—so you constantly have to choose which of the two to follow. A woman once confessed to me that this makes her feel like her brain is about to explode. I feel the same way.

Music is pretty much the raison d'être of dancing. It's why we dance differently to different types of music. So why oh why do so many tango dancers treat musicality as an afterthought?

I believe there are two reasons:

First, there is no basic step in tango. In most social dances, there is a basic step that fits a specific rhythmic pattern and generally adheres cleanly to a musical phrase. Let's again use salsa as an example. In salsa, you have three steps, a pause, then three more steps and a pause, all of which fit perfectly into an eight-count phrase. So the basic step is taught as a pattern that starts and ends in time with each musical phrase. But in tango, there is no real basic step besides the walk, so you are not obliged to start a sequence on "1" or finish on "8." Even if we do use some sequences as part of our vocabulary—and some of those might even contain exactly eight steps or actions—we can change the rhythmic pattern by pausing for a beat or two or dancing double-time, thereby changing the place in the music where we complete our figure. Add to that the unpredictability of our partner's responses and the traffic on the dance floor, and it becomes impossible to impose any type of sequence with a specific step count or musical count.

Second, tango music is so layered that there are many ways to interpret and play with it. It's hard for teachers to impose a musical structure on their students when so many other musical structures might work just as well: quick-quick-slow, slow-slow-slow, slow-quick-quick—not to mention adding pauses or syncopation. But I think teachers do need to pick one pattern and impose it at first, as an exercise in awareness and discipline. We need to train students to dance to the music, to consistently keep time with the beat. Because so many just don't. They figure they'll worry about the steps first and deal with following the music later. But often that "later" never comes; they get so used to dancing to the beat of their own drum—or ignoring it altogether—that they never learn to let the music lead them and inspire them.

There are different levels of musicality for dancers:

The beat. Also called the pulse, this is the basic unit of time in the music. It is the rhythm you would tap your toes or clap your hands to. In tango, it is your basic walking rhythm: Your walk follows the regular strong, or accented, beats in the music. The beat, or *el compás*, is like an ever-present metronome; it is the constant and consistent time that all the musicians are keeping, even as their melodies speed up, slow down, or pause. Like a heartbeat, it is always present, whether you hear it or not. In other types of music, this time is often played by a drum or other percussion instrument. This is rarely the case in Argentine tango, however. In fact, different instruments can play the beat at different times, which is one of the reasons it's hard for some people to even hear (or feel) the beat in tango at first. It's a challenge for some, but it's essential for all. You can't be on the music if you can't find the beat—so find it and force yourself to stick to it before moving on to other possibilities.

Some people think that teachers should bypass lessons about dancing on the beat and instead instruct students to dance on the melody or just the "feeling" of the music. I disagree. I have seen too many dancers who have trouble even hearing the beat consistently, let alone dancing to it, so I think it's important to teach this basic concept first. If you're on the beat, you will not be wrong, although you will eventually want to make things more interesting by playing with . . .

Pauses and double-time. In terms of variation on the beat, **pauses** will come first: Often, you'll have no choice but to stop moving for a beat or two. You might do this to get your bearings, to let your partner get theirs, or to manage the always unpredictable dance-floor traffic. Just be sure you pause for a beat or two or three—not some random time that ignores the music. Pause on a beat and start again on a beat. **Double-time dancing,** sometimes called *traspié* (especially in *milonga*) or *contratiempo,* means dancing twice as fast. In other words, you're doing three steps in two musical beats. This is where things get interesting—and, of course, more challenging. Just remember, if you can't yet stick to the time, you won't be able to handle double-time.

Syncopation, phrasing, and dancing the melody. These are more complex concepts. They're great fun for high-level dancers because you can get incredibly creative. But that means they're also quite difficult. Many dancers never get to the point where they can use these elements, and you absolutely need to master the previous concepts before attempting to go further.

- **Syncopation.** This means placing rhythmic stresses or accents where they wouldn't normally occur. Generally, this would be done where the musicians are doing it. That means you have to hear it, get your feet to mark it, and get your partner to feel it—all in the space of a fraction of a beat.
- **Phrasing.** This is the way the music is grouped into structures. In tango, these structures will usually be 8 or 16 counts. You don't have to "start on 1" the way you do in some other dances, but be aware that the music changes between phrases. If you're cognizant of the phrasing and the changes, you can also change the quality of your dancing in those moments. This makes your dancing more fully connected to and expressive of the music.
- **Dancing the melody.** The melody is the part of the music you would sing or hum; it's what makes each song identifiable. You could dance the melody by dancing the way you would sing the music, by marking the intricate rhythmic sequences of one of the instruments, or by dancing the "feeling" of the music. This is what will, or should, make us dance differently to different orchestras. It's partly instinctual. From the time my children were young, they would dance to different genres of music in different ways: country, swing, hip hop, classical . . . But the fascinating thing is that their moves would closely resemble the dances associated with each of those genres. It didn't matter if they'd never heard the music or seen the dance before. Their knowledge was innate. Each style of music automatically evokes a different feeling and a particular

way of expressing it physically. If we extend this concept to tango, it means that the feeling and quality of our dancing should change with each *tanda*, each style, each orchestra. It's obvious that *vals* should be danced differently from *milonga*, that *milonga* should be danced differently from tango—but within these styles each orchestra should be danced differently as well. If you wouldn't move the same way to Tchaikovsky as to Eminem, would you dance a 1930s rhythmic D'Arienzo the same way as a dramatic Pugliese from the '50s?

As you can see, dancing to music is as complex as music itself. So what is the follower's role in all of this? There's a mistaken idea that musicality is mainly the leader's job. But like everything else in tango, it should be 50/50.

First, the music will inspire the follower's embellishments. Why do I choose a tap versus a *lápiz*? A series of tiny, playful steps versus a slow caress of my partner's leg? The music, of course! Second, sometimes it's the follower's job to keep the time. For example, if my partner leads me a turn while he pivots on one foot and embellishes with difficult *enrosques*, it's up to me to mark the rhythm with my steps. By doing this, I will help him to turn, maintain his balance, and easily keep track of where I am so he can end the turn at just the right moment.

The music has another important role in couple dancing: It is a synchronization tool. If my partner and I are both dancing to the same music, we will more easily dance in sync with each other. When going beyond the beat to dance double-time, to syncopate, or to explore other layers of rhythm and melody, it is essential for the follower to be as in tune with the music as the leader. For example, when my leader wants me to dance double-time, he gives me a lead to go faster. But what tells me exactly how fast to go? The music! My leader doesn't place my foot on the floor; I do, and I do it to the music. If he wants me to syncopate or mark a more intricate melodic pattern? It's impossible if I'm not hearing this in the music myself.

If all of this sounds daunting, remember: Start with the basics, or the beat, and you will not go wrong. As you master one concept, you can attempt the next. Maybe one day you will embody the music, using your own body like one of the instruments in the orchestra; you will keep time with the beat while filling the space in between with melodies full of creativity, emotion, and suspense.

So musicality might just be the most important element in our dancing. Then again, you do need steps.

~ Lesson 10 ~

YES, YOU DO NEED STEPS

If there are no predefined figures or steps in Argentine tango dancing, why do most teachers teach sequences, or figures? It seems contradictory, but it's not.

If tango is a language, it's all well and good to know the rules of grammar, spelling, and punctuation, but you can't apply any of them if you have no vocabulary to work with. This is why teachers teach steps and sequences—all the while insisting that they're secondary to stuff like connection, musicality, and technique.

When we learn a new language, we usually learn a few key phrases to start us off: "Hello, my name is Andrea. What is your name?" or "How much does this cost?" or "Would you like to dance?" We can use these to start communicating on a basic level immediately. After that, we can go back and learn the alphabet, the rules of grammar, syntax, and so on. The ultimate goal is to be able to formulate our own sentences and speak fluently. If we one day master the language, we won't have to think about how it all works anymore.

Tango is much the same. We get a few simple sequences to work with in the form of structures (phrases) we can learn, practise, and understand. We use those to communicate while working on the individual movements (the alphabet) and technique (grammar, syntax, etc.). Eventually, we may be able to create new sequences on the fly (prose) while retaining our connection (conversation) with our partner and playing with the music (poetry!).

If we've learned to walk with a partner in front of us, we're already communicating at a basic level, but we need a certain amount of vocabulary to really express ourselves. However, just as fancy vocabulary alone doesn't make for great conversation, fancy moves alone don't make a great dancer. Still, cool moves are, well, cool, and as long as you use them correctly and in the right context, they are an essential—not to mention fun—part of dancing tango.

Sequences are both pedagogical tools and leading tools, and that's why I believe they're an unavoidable part of the teaching/learning process. But it's important for instructors to make the following things clear: "Sequences" are different from individual "movements," and in the end it's the mastery of the movements that counts most. The sequences are a means to an end, not the end itself.

We use sequences to teach such fundamental moves as steps and pivots, which when put together become such mini-structures as walking sequences, *ochos* and *giros*, which when linked with transitional steps become what we think of as figures. Teaching a movement within the context of a sequence gives useful points of reference to tango students.

Followers don't need to remember the sequences, but they do need to learn them, understand them, and practise them. Getting stuck on the idea of the sequence itself will encourage anticipation on the part of followers; they will be overly concerned with what comes next. But practising sequences and understanding how the individual parts fit together teaches their bodies to do what they need to do. Students will learn how it should feel when their steps are properly synchronized to their partners'.

It would be great if we could just teach improvisation from the start—if we could get beginners to see the big picture from Day One, skipping the difficult, cumbersome, and often frustrating aspects of learning. But we can't bypass the early parts of the process, because learning tango is just that: a *process*. And it goes something like this:

1. We learn some basic moves, sequences, techniques, and leading and following tools. All of these will feel awkward and surprisingly difficult at first; nothing will really seem much like dancing yet.

2. We learn some more moves and sequences while trying to master the first ones. We also pay more attention to posture, the music, and a bunch of other stuff that still feels like too much to think about all at once. This creates confusion and frustration for leaders, who have a tough enough time learning and remembering their own steps,

let alone knowing what their partner is doing every second. On top of all that, leaders have to wrap their minds and bodies around concepts such as parallel versus cross system. It's a lot! Meanwhile, followers may feel that they're learning faster than their partners. In fact, they may start to feel they can really dance—if they get paired with a more advanced leader or teacher. At this stage, both partners are often impatient with the leader's learning pace.

3. Leaders continue to feel stressed out about not knowing enough moves. They also get bored with themselves if they don't execute every move they've ever learned within a single song. Followers start to understand that their role involves more than following. They begin to realize that they should be responsible for their own axis, steps, and pivots, and they begin to grasp that not every mistake is the leader's fault. Teachers keep saying that both partners should be focusing more on posture, connection, musicality, and floorcraft, but most intermediate-level dancers don't yet fully understand this or believe it. Leaders and followers can feel stuck in a rut at this point; they both realize how much there is to learn and that it will take more time and hard work.

4. Leaders and followers both experience some "Aha!" moments where, by fluke or design, everything comes together with ease: steps, balance, comfy embrace, and the perfect moment in the music. At this point, leaders have been exposed to just about every type of move that has a name—*ochos, giros, paradas, barridas, sacadas, ganchos, boleos, volcadas, colgadas*. Having spent a fair amount of time dancing in *milongas*, leaders also realize that as they improve their embrace, posture, and musicality, things

work better more often. Meanwhile, followers stop need-
ing to be led into endless series of impressive moves to
enjoy a dance. They start to derive more and more pleasure from a good embrace, creative musicality, and simple
steps. They appreciate how these give them a chance to
connect, embellish, play with the music, and express
themselves.

5. Those years of hard work are paying off, and both leaders
and followers understand that it all starts with a good
connection and moves on from there. The sequences and
moves become tools for improvising with the music and
their partners. Skill and enjoyment become more about
the *how*, not the *what*. At this point, dancers look back
and wish they had understood what it's all about sooner.
Though they've reached a stage where onlookers consider
them advanced, they see that the tango learning process
is an endless journey. While they derive satisfaction from
knowing how far they have come, they only want to go
further still.

Yes, it's a process. But it's a magnificent journey, too.

~ Lesson 11 ~

THE TRUTH IS . . . ELUSIVE

The truth may be out there, but I have not yet found it, and you would have a hard time convincing me anyone else has.

During my two decades of seeking the great truth about tango, I have found many small truths. Some of these, on the surface, seem to contradict each other: Connection is the most important thing; technique is the most important thing. Embrace is everything; musicality is everything. Steps first, then technique; technique first, then steps. No sequences, just improvisation; sequences first, then improvisation! Focus on your hands and feet and the rest will come; focus on your centre and the rest will come. The key to good posture is the position of the pelvis; the key to good posture is the position of the shoulder blades . . .

Seeking the truth is like seeking the perfect teaching method. While every teacher believes he or she has the best method, the truth is that most teachers' methods evolve over time. I can tell you from experience that at each stage of that evolution, we feel we have grasped a new, great truth. But a month, a year, or 10 years later, those truths have transformed yet again. Does that mean we were wrong last year and are now finally right? We probably think so, but so does the teacher across town who has just discovered his own new truth.

Some teachers are dead set against teaching any type of "basic step" or other pre-formatted sequence. Others don't believe in teaching technique, because they think students will develop good technique on their own through the repetition of movements and sequences. There are teachers, dancers, and even choreographers who don't believe in counting and only use musical cues. They say the counting makes your dancing too mechanical—that you should feel the music and your dancing will be musical. Makes sense. But then there are those who need to count everything. They say if you learn to structure your dancing to the music, the "feeling" will come with time. Makes sense, too. Is one approach better or more "true"?

In reality, an approach that's right for one person could be all wrong for another. Different people learn differently. This means teachers need to take various approaches to instruction and students need to find teachers who fit their own learning style.

While a visual learner might benefit most from watching a teacher demonstrate a movement several times, an auditory learner might prefer a detailed breakdown and explanation. A kinesthetic learner will be eager to try the steps themselves and will want to copy the teachers as they demonstrate. Detail-oriented types will pick things up differently than those who quickly see the big picture. Each type of student will benefit from a particular teaching approach. They will also probably hone their various skill sets in a different order. But none of this is set in stone. A student who starts off as an auditory learner might find they can benefit from a more kinesthetic approach later on.

In the end, the best approach to both teaching and dancing probably includes a little of everything: technique, fun steps, demonstrations, explanations... and practice and time, of course.

Now, there are also divided camps when it comes to musical taste: "Everything after 1955 is worthless!" versus "More than two Golden Age *tandas* in a row is boring and repetitive!" I can tell you that both camps feel strongly about their taste and each is pretty much convinced they know the truth about tango music. So whose musical taste is right? Well, I always think of a certain dancer I know. His tastes are generally traditional (Fresedo-Ray, D'Agostino-Vargas, Laurenz, Maffia), he knows his tango orchestras better than most, he loves the Golden Age classics and rolls his eyes when something big and dramatic like Varela comes on—but then he has no problem dancing to one of my totally alternative *tandas,* like Tom Waits.

So we've covered different kinds of teachers, different kinds of students, and different kinds of music. But what about different kinds of dancers? The overall tango experience itself is not the same for everyone. I can divide tango dancers into three main groups: social dancers, performers, and perpetual students.

Social dancers. Since tango is primarily a social dance, social dancers are by far the predominant group. Within this group we find all sorts, but I will divide people into two subgroups: *gourmands* and *gourmets*.

A *gourmand* considers a successful night to be one during which almost no *tandas* are sat out. These dancers are on the dance floor as much as possible, dancing with as many partners as possible, rarely sitting down to chat and almost never heading to the bar for a drink. This all-you-can-dance buffet type of dancer is often looked down on by the more discerning *gourmet* dancers.

Gourmets always aim for quality over quantity. They dance to select *tandas* with select partners, are sticklers for the *códigos* (codes of conduct), and spend as much time mingling among themselves as actually dancing. They are often highly skilled and therefore pretty convinced they've got it right, but others accuse them of exclusion, snobbery, and elitism. Whoever is right, social dancers all forget that there are different kinds of tango dancers.

Performers. Some professional dancers spend so much time training, touring, and performing that they rarely make an appearance at *milongas*. Of these performers, *escenario* (stage) dancers in particular are often dismissed by social dancers. Their style of dancing is considered too choreographed, flashy, or acrobatic to be "true" tango. But these dancers have skills well beyond what the rest of us can ever hope to achieve. So who among us is the true tango dancer?

Perpetual students. Speaking of dancers who don't go to *milongas*, I have students who have taken regular lessons for years but who never go out to dance socially—even if they're quite proficient. Perhaps they have lifestyles (children, career, nondancing life partner) that don't lend themselves to weekends and late nights spent in tango clubs, or perhaps the tango social scene just doesn't appeal to them even though they love the music and the learning process. Is such a person less of a tango dancer?

The thing is, *all* these dancers are tango dancers, even if their skills, goals, visions, and experience levels are vastly different.

I guess the truth about tango lies somewhere in the balance between simple fun and hard work, cool moves and strong technique, discipline and creativity, tradition and evolution. There may not be one great truth, but the quest will lead to many great discoveries.

~ Lesson 12 ~

YOU NEED A THICK SKIN TO DANCE TANGO

If you're reading this, you probably love tango—but you probably also know that it's not as easy as you thought. I'm not just talking about remembering sequences, honing your technique, or following the rhythm, either. This lesson is about the ways in which tango can be unkind to your ego and self-esteem.

As a student of tango

Tango is a social dance, and we say it's a dance for everyone. You've most certainly heard that if you can walk, you can dance tango. That's my own school's motto, and while I stand by it, I must admit that just because you can walk doesn't mean you can dance tango *well*. This is a fact that all dancers must face if they are to improve and advance.

After a few lessons, we begin to realize that the very simplicity of tango is what makes it difficult. Tango is a delicate balance full of paradoxes and contradictions. It takes clarity and subtlety, an embrace that is both soft and firm, legs that are at once powerful and free, knees that are extended yet mobile. While social tango doesn't require extreme flexibility and isn't an intense cardiovascular workout, it does take strength, balance, and good posture. It also takes awareness of our partner and those around us, which means we need good communication and listening skills. And it takes a lot of body awareness. The thing is, people often don't even know that they lack body awareness. Realizing how little you know your own body can be a blow to the ego.

Tango is the ultimate exercise in multi-tasking: You must coordinate your every move to the music, your partner, and the couples around you on the dance floor; you must do all this while constantly planning your next move and being ready to react and change that plan at any moment; and you must make it all look and feel effortless. Sounds like a lot, and it is.

But this is the beauty of tango, and it's the reason it is so rewarding when we finally start to get it. It's also the reason you can dance tango for years and never get bored. There is always room for improvement—a better embrace, straighter posture, stronger steps and pivots. And then there's the music. There are so many layers to tango music and so many possibilities for tango dancers. As beginners, we often don't hear or appreciate the subtleties of the different orchestras (even if we love tango music). But the longer we dance and the more we listen, the more we can explore the intricacies of the music. The most advanced and musically proficient dancers never tire of the Golden Age classics because there are always new layers to play with and rediscover.

My advice is to appreciate every step of the eternal learning process that is tango. I think this is the key to not getting so frustrated that you give up when you realize how difficult it really is. Notice how you reap the benefits of your hard work both on and off the dance floor: Maybe you stand straighter in your daily life or walk down the street with more self-assurance; perhaps you've suddenly become better at listening to other people. Remember to look back and realize how far you've come. When you catch yourself looking ahead and feeling overwhelmed by all there is left to learn, see it as a gift that you will keep on giving yourself. If the learning process is never-ending, that means the rewards are never-ending, too.

As a social dancer

Socially, tango is about human interaction and connections. If you like tango, then you probably seek out these interactions and enjoy them on the whole. But not all of them will be positive, of course. It takes all kinds to make a tango world, so while every encounter will be marvellously different, not every encounter will be marvellous. Here are a couple of unpleasant phenomena you've probably already experienced and will experience again.

Teachy partners. Unfortunately, this one comes up a lot. People do it, people complain about it and I have to deal with it. If you know me or my writing, you already know that teaching on the dance floor is a pet peeve of mine. Teachy behaviour includes any type of comment or feedback on our partner's dancing, from the embrace to the walk to a lead for a particular move. It also includes non-verbal adjustments to our partner's embrace or posture, such as placing their hand differently or pushing their shoulders down. Advice, feedback, corrections—it all falls into the same category.

Teachy behaviour is all about the ego: The perpetrator is automatically assuming that the other person is the problem. Getting over this behaviour requires admitting that we are at least 50 percent of the problem, which is not an easy thing for our ego to accept.

Of course, being the recipient of dance-floor teaching is hard on the ego as well. We may feel angry, hurt, defensive, inferior, insecure, or simply annoyed—and understandably so. Not to mention that corrections and comments interrupt the flow of a dance, breaking any pleasant, enjoy-the-moment connection there might have been.

Teaching, correcting, or adjusting our partner during a *milonga* is totally unacceptable in my book. However, we will all be confronted with it at some point. When faced with this behaviour, what can we do? I suggest remaining silent and neutral after the first comment or adjustment. But if the corrections continue, say something. Non-confrontational "I" statements usually work best: "I prefer not to talk when I'm dancing." If the behaviour persists, feel free to say "thank you" after the song and end the *tanda* early. If your partner is offended or asks why, be direct. I can't tell you how many people have stormed out or come to me in tears after being corrected and condescended to on the dance floor. The perpetrators need to be made aware that their behaviour is hurtful and unacceptable.

If you're a beginner and your partner is more experienced, do not encourage this type of behaviour by asking for feedback on the *milonga* dance floor. Accept yourself at the level you are at and realize you're allowed to just relax and enjoy, even if you're not yet "advanced." If you really think your partner is qualified to offer useful feedback, you can ask during a *práctica* or during a conversation off the dance floor. Even then, unless you're speaking to an actual teacher, take any advice with a grain of salt.

Remember that the constant need to teach or fix one's partner says more about the "teacher" than the "student." In tango, as in life, when things aren't going as planned, we should first look at how we can adjust ourselves to improve the situation. Just dance, accept the person in your arms as they are in the moment, take advantage of their strengths, and don't dwell on their weaknesses. After all, you have some, too.

Feeling rejected. Sometimes you don't get to dance much, and sometimes you don't get to dance with the person or people you were hoping to dance with. Talk about a blow to your ego and self-esteem.

When you get all dressed up and hyped for a night that doesn't meet your expectations, it kind of sucks. But no matter who you are or what your skill level is, it will happen to you now and again. I have bad nights, too. Sometimes I feel overlooked and rejected and wonder why none of my *miradas* are working. When this happens, I go home deflated and grumpy.

Luckily, there are always good nights to balance out the bad. I've gained enough life experience and perspective to know that often the bad nights are more about my outlook than about reality. And sometimes bad nights just happen—for all kinds of reasons. Did women outnumber men? Was I tucked away in a corner or frequently absorbed in conversation?

That being said, if you feel you're consistently overlooked, maybe it's time to work on your skills. Yes, I believe advanced dancers should be a little more generous with issuing and accepting invitations, but I also believe it's normal to stick with people we know we'll enjoy dancing with. So if you want to get more dances, work on becoming a joy to dance with. If we all prioritized our partners' enjoyment rather than our own, we would all receive more enjoyment in the end.

Finally, remember that a *milonga* is not only about dancing as many *tandas* as possible; it is also about meeting friends, hearing beautiful music, and admiring the other dancers. Rather than focusing on every *tanda* we sit out, we should soak up the whole atmosphere of an evening. We might have a great night even if we don't dance that much, and we might also radiate more positive energy, seem more approachable, and eventually end up dancing more.

As a couple

Tango can be hard on couples. We'll only touch briefly on this topic for now, as we'll explore it in depth in a later lesson. Suffice it to say that many of the issues couples face in tango boil down to two things: jealousy and different learning paces. I don't believe that tango causes relationship problems, but it sure can amplify existing ones.

This is definitely the case when it comes to jealousy. If you're new to tango, it can be disconcerting to see the love of your life in the arms of someone else—and enjoying it. But once you really understand tango, you'll see that it's all about the dance and nothing more. The intensity, connection, and abandon don't leave the dance floor. If someone is looking for more than the dance, this has nothing to do with tango itself; tango may just be the chosen avenue. If your life partnership is strong and you trust your partner, tango won't be a problem. If your relationship is fragile and you don't trust your partner, tango may be a dangerous game to play, but it is not to blame.

Then there is the frustration that comes with learning tango together. Remember, people pick things up at different paces. Either partner might be a quicker study, but often it is the leader who receives the brunt of the blame, impatience, and frustration—from both parties.

It's generally accepted that the early stages of the learning curve are hardest for leaders. There's a lot to think about and understand right from the start. Meanwhile, followers with a few natural following skills can feel they dance well pretty quickly if paired with an experienced leader. So both partners feel—somewhat mistakenly—that the follower is learning faster or dancing better than her partner. As a result, both get impatient with the leader's learning pace. Reality sets in later for the followers, once they realize there is so much more to their role than "just following." All of this is normal, so try to remember to be patient and generous toward your partner. You're both learning and trying your best.

In tango, as in life, nothing can be positive all the time, no matter how much you love it. The hard moments are there to teach us, and the great moments are there to reward us. It's all about balance. Without the difficult times, we would not savour the good ones as much.

If you stick to tango and work hard, you will improve. Perhaps you'll even break that elusive "advanced" barrier one day. Along the way there will be dips and plateaus in the learning process, frustration, refusals, insecurity, jealousy, awkward moments, and bad nights. Your ego and self-esteem will get hit again and again.

All of this still happens to me, and I have hard days when I think maybe I should just give it all up. But I don't, of course. Because tango does so much for me, including thickening my skin with a little tough love from time to time.

~ Lesson 13 ~

EVERYONE SHOULD LEARN TO
LEAD AND FOLLOW

How can you become a better dancer while connecting more completely to your partners? By learning to both express *and* listen, to give *and* take. You can acquire these skills by learning to lead *and* follow, regardless of your initial or preferred role.

Technique is technique, connection is connection. While there is some mental difference between the two roles—leaders need to plan and navigate and have a certain understanding of their partner's steps in a way that followers do not—there is little to no difference in the body.

Before we go further, let me offer this piece of advice: Don't try to change your technique when you change roles. By all means, improve your posture, your embrace, your musicality, and anything else you need to work on. But know that whatever you improve will apply to whichever role you are dancing.

Now, some people are afraid they'll hinder their dancing by exploring the other role. I think this is rare, and those who do run into problems are probably too hung up on the "leader" versus "follower" terminology to begin with. In fact, I find these terms limiting, problematic, even detrimental. These simple words make some dancers resistant to learning the other role, and they don't convey what the two roles are really about—or how much they actually have in common. (For further discussion, see "Tango terminology" at the end of this book.) In short, leading and following each contain a good dose of the other already, and the best dancers use both elements to their advantage. The best leaders are receptive and the strongest followers are expressive. Working on both qualities will likely enhance an important aspect of your dancing: playfulness.

A potential solution is for teachers to teach both roles to everyone from the start. Some do this, and I think it's an interesting approach. It's not *my* approach, however, and here's why: First, most students who come through the door don't want to learn both roles—yet. Second, it would mean revamping my entire teaching structure to an extent I am not ready for—yet. Third, I'm not convinced that teaching both roles from the get-go is necessarily better than teaching one role at a time—yet.

But maybe I'll come around to the idea. For now, I believe both methods have their strong points and neither is ideal for everyone.

In any case, I think it's generally accepted that learning to follow improves leading skills. How could it not? Since leaders need to understand their partners' steps and movements, it makes sense to actually learn them. To paraphrase a well-known saying, the best way to experience someone else's reality is to walk a mile in their shoes.

The reverse—that followers will improve by learning to lead—is not so generally accepted. There is a myth among some male leaders that women who learn to lead damage their following skills. Men who believe this even claim to have anecdotal evidence to back up their assertion. Sorry, guys, but I don't buy it. Teachers are among the most highly skilled dancers, and most if not all of them dance both roles. I know that learning to lead has contributed greatly to my overall dance skills and therefore to my following skills.

It's true, however, that a follower's connection with their partners may suffer temporarily. Learning a new role, like learning any new technique, takes work and mental effort. While we're in the process of perfecting something unfamiliar, we may be distracted by and focused on the new skill. It's exactly what all beginner leaders go through when they're too busy figuring out the steps and trying to navigate the floor to really connect or *dance*. But once a follower has the basics of the leader role down—and perhaps more importantly, once they believe they know what they're doing—they can let go and think about their partner.

Female leaders also receive criticism for their navigational skills, with some male leaders complaining that women are hazardous "drivers." Again, part of that comes down to where they are on the leading learning curve. Sure, there are female leaders who are dangerous and don't respect the *ronda,* but there are plenty of erratic male "drivers" as well; they just don't stand out as much because they blend in with the majority. I guess this is a good place to remind everyone that floorcraft and line of dance should not be an afterthought; they're just as important as dance moves and musicality. When we learn to drive a car, it's vital to learn how the vehicle itself functions. However, it's just as vital to learn how to follow the flow of traffic and make safe turns. The same should be true on the dance floor. Regardless of your gender, I say to all leaders: Build your navigational skills and dance with respect for those around you.

Some people love dancing both leader and follower roles, while some have a strong preference for one or the other. I enjoy leading and have worked hard to build strong leading skills over the years, but I just don't experience the same bliss leading as I do following. I relish the sense of abandon in my primary role. When I lead, I'm much more in my head, and I get enough of that in my daily life, I guess!

So I'm not saying that everyone must master both roles or dance them equally. What I *am* saying is that we all should experiment at some point to develop at least a minimal understanding of what our partners feel and need. And who knows, if you try it, you might be surprised at how much you like it.

~ Lesson 14 ~

HOW TO BREAK THAT ADVANCED BARRIER

In the tango learning process, the intermediate level is the toughest, the longest-lasting, and the hardest to break out of. Really? But wouldn't the beginner level be harder than the intermediate stage? Not in my opinion. There's a reason why most dancers out there are intermediate.

The beginner phase

As beginners, we're in a place of pure discovery; you could call it tango innocence. This tango world is all new and somewhat magical. Sure, there's some frustration at this stage, but most dancers move along the learning curve pretty quickly at the start, going from nothing to something in a short time.

I would say the beginner stage lasts somewhere between six months and a year for the average tango student—but there are always exceptions. Every few years, a particularly gifted student skyrockets from beginner to advanced in a year. On the flip side, there are students who repeat Tango 1 half a dozen times without ever really getting it. But for the most part, students acquire enough skill and knowledge within a year to move on to the next stage.

The intermediate phase

At this point, tango has lost some of that initial mystery. We still love it, we're still impressed by those who have mastered it, but it's no longer brand new or unattainable in the way that it once was.

This stage is full of plateaus in the learning curve. Just as we feel we're getting somewhere, we have a crappy night and decide we don't know a thing after all. There is frustration. Lots of frustration.

At this stage, leaders tend to feel stressed out about not knowing enough moves, and they get bored with themselves if they don't execute loads of them during a *tanda*. Followers get frustrated, too—with their partners if they feel they're not keeping up, and with themselves as they realize not every mistake is the leader's fault. The follower learns that their side of the partnership is more difficult than they expected. While this realization is a good sign, again, it's frustrating.

Meanwhile, teachers keep saying to focus more on posture, connection, musicality, and floorcraft, but most intermediate-level dancers don't yet fully grasp these concepts. Leaders and followers can both feel in a rut as they clue in to how much more time and hard work lie ahead. Many dancers stop really moving forward at this point. They have enough moves and partners to enjoy themselves at *milongas*, so why keep putting time, sweat, and money into classes? If the goal was to socialize and dance, it has been reached. Many dancers are content here and don't feel the need to take things further.

Some, however, do want to go further; they want to break through the next barrier and become truly "advanced." Most dancers at the high end of the intermediate phase have hovered at the cusp at least a few times, experiencing nights when, by fluke or design, everything comes together with ease: steps, balance, embrace, and the perfect moment in the music. They feel what it should be, what it could be, and they want more. These dancers need to find a way to fully break through or they may give up in frustration.

For all but the most exceptional dancers (who are few and far between), the intermediate stage lasts the longest. On average, it begins at around one year, and for many it never ends. This is not to say there is no improvement in all this time; the intermediate level is wide-ranging and most dancers advance at least somewhat. But actually breaking the elusive "advanced" barrier will not happen for everyone, no matter how many *milongas* you attend.

The advanced phase

Once we become truly advanced, we find new magic. We finally understand all these things we heard about before but never really got. It's like being admitted to a secret society and unlocking new levels of enlightenment. We dance with abandon, embody the music, become one with our partners. There are still and forever new discoveries to come, but they are on a whole different plane.

Those years of hard work are paying off and it is so rewarding. This is when the light comes on and we understand for ourselves what our teachers have been saying all along: Technique is king and will free us to enjoy the dance on a whole new level. We see that the sequences and moves are secondary not just to technique but to musicality, connection, floorcraft. Now we really comprehend that both skill and enjoyment are about the how, not the what.

It is rare for a dancer to become truly advanced in less than five years, and, as I said before, many never really do.

I wish I had the universal, magic solution to achieving this breakthrough, but I don't. In the end, the hard work and resulting accomplishments belong to each dancer. As a teacher, I can only guide and coach; I can't do the work for you. I can steer you in the right direction and even lead you along the right path, but whether you reach your destination or not is up to you.

That said, I can suggest the following recipe—but you have to put it together.

Four essential ingredients to achieve that breakthrough:

1. **Talent.** Some people walk in the door and their teachers just know they have something special. They move right,

absorb corrections almost instantly, and seem to get the big picture from the start. Maybe she had dance training all her life and developed strength, axis, and body awareness early on. Maybe he's not a musician or a dancer (yet), but he just "has it in his blood" and moves like he was born on the dance floor. If you've got talent like this, the rest will be easier. Then again, many people take their talent for granted and are lazy students because of it. So talent helps for sure, but alone it is no guarantee of greatness—in tango or elsewhere.

2. **Hard work.** This means you train regularly outside the *milonga* setting. **First, you continue to take lessons**, especially private ones. I would say that every single person who has reached the advanced level has studied privately with a good teacher at some point. **Second, you incorporate workouts besides tango** in order to improve things like posture, balance, and strength. This could mean yoga classes, working with a personal trainer, or something else. Remember that body awareness, correct alignment, good posture, and strong legs are essential to mastering tango. **Third, you remain humble enough to admit that you are never done learning.** No matter how good you get, you could get better. There is this phenomenon in social dance of students stopping their classes in local studios after just a year or two. This is not the case in such disciplines as ballet or yoga, in which even advanced practitioners continue to attend classes for years and years. So why do the vast majority of tango dancers take a few sessions of regular classes and then suddenly turn their noses up at the local studios' offerings? Why do they instead opt only for festival classes taught by travelling maestros—if they continue with any classes at all? Don't get me wrong,

I take advantage of these opportunities, too. But they're pricey and offer no follow-up, so they're probably less valuable as a learning tool for your average dancer than regular lessons with a quality teacher. That said, once you've finally broken that advanced barrier, you can actually start learning a lot on your own. You'll have such an integral understanding of your own body and what constitutes good tango technique that you can train on your own or with a partner and improve through a certain amount of self-teaching. You can practise without the constant observations of a teacher because you are practising *right*. But, as any advanced dancer knows, periodic lessons and coaching from a maestro or teaching colleague are a must. Even the best dancers have bad habits and sometimes need an outsider to point them out.

3. **Determination.** You have to want it and be willing to work for it. This can't come from anyone but you. Some people don't necessarily feel this determination early on, but one day, for whatever reason, they suddenly wake up wanting to "get there." They will do the hard work necessary, spurred on by its rewards rather than discouraged by its demands. This decisive action is essential.

4. **Time.** Years of experience alone will not make you advanced. We all know people who have been dancing for 15 years but whose technique has not budged in the last 10. Still, you can't rush the process, either. Your mind and body need time to integrate and absorb the work you do. While practising tango three times a week will certainly be more effective than once a week, taking 10 classes a week and dancing every single night won't necessarily accelerate your learning pace exponentially. So put in the floor time but accept that it will also just take time.

You need to find just the right blend of hard work, time, and determination. Add to that a pinch of talent and you're cooking.

~ Lesson 15 ~

ASSERT YOURSELF

I was a shy kid and an insecure teenager. It took me decades to learn how to be assertive, to say no, to stand up for myself, and to ask for what I want. Tango is one of the things that has helped me along this road. It has shown me how important a quality decisiveness is—in dance and in life.

On the dance floor

The benefits of being clear about what you want seem kind of obvious when it comes to leading, but followers need to be clear, too.

Let's start with leaders. If *you* don't know what you want, your follower certainly won't. Hesitation breeds hesitation, so if you constantly wait to see if your partner is going to follow, she will be in a perpetual state of doubt—and so will the dance. No one said leading is easy: You have to simultaneously wait for your partner and show her where to go next, which means you have to actually *know* where you want to go next. Although things don't always go according to plan in tango, you still need to *have* a plan and state it clearly (with actions, not words). Otherwise, the dance will be sloppy rather than spontaneous.

Also, if you don't know where you want each step to land or pivot to end—be it your own or your partner's—you will have little control over your line of dance and the space you take up on the floor. This will put your partner in danger and annoy the dancers around you.

Let's move on to followers. If I have one piece of advice, it's this: Do not be passive. Embrace your partner the way you want to be embraced, dance the music the way you feel it, take the time you need to complete each movement before going to the next. Own your dance and you will be both more fulfilled by it *and* more fulfilling to dance with.

This advice might sound like "Do whatever you want." That's not it at all. Everything the follower does must be within the framework created by the leader and the music. But within that framework there is so much room to express yourself and to *dance*.

And you must do just that. Dance. Don't hesitate, wonder, question, worry. Accept each movement, each reaction, and mean it. If there was a miscommunication, it's too late to fix it anyway, so just take the step and move on from there. Believe you know what to do and you will follow more, not less, because you will clear away all that worry and hesitation, allowing you to receive your leader's messages with less interference. Your leader will receive your messages more clearly, too. He'll listen more, and the *tanda* will be a fascinating conversation rather than a monologue.

Off the dance floor

The way you carry yourself conveys a lot. If you walk into a room with poise and determination, you will get noticed; if you sit and stand up straight, you will look like you know how to dance before you even hit the floor. I've heard more than one maestro say that you need to be a tango dancer from the moment you step through the front door. Posture affects not only how you appear but also how you feel. Simply lifting and opening up the chest can alleviate feelings of depression, for example. If you stand tall, you may end up feeling more confident. Hold yourself like a dancer and you will look and feel like one. You'll likely receive more *miradas* and *cabeceos* as well.

I'm a relatively recent convert to the *mirada-cabeceo* invitation system, but I'm a big supporter of it. *Mirada* means "look," *cabeceo* means "nod," and together they make up the traditional, non-verbal, and most widely accepted way of inviting and getting invited to dance tango. Basically, leader and follower look directly at the person they hope to dance with and, hopefully, catch each other's eye. Then the leader nods or motions with his or her head and the follower nods or smiles his or her acceptance.

Find the whole idea daunting? You're not alone. Because I still have a shy, insecure person living inside me, I found this one hard to master at first. Okay, I still do sometimes.

Once I get on the dance floor, I know what I'm doing. Off the floor, however, it's tough for me to assert myself by looking directly into someone's eyes—especially a stranger. So I get that it's not necessarily an easy system. But neither is tango. And if you can learn this complex dance, you can learn this simple exchange.

It's worth it because it works. You're not sitting around passively waiting to be chosen by whomever decides to walk up to you and ask; you're not hovering around and making someone else uncomfortable; and you're not asking directly and risking outright rejection or a reluctant "yes" from someone who doesn't really want to dance with you but doesn't want to hurt your feelings.

The *mirada-cabeceo* system works because it is assertive on both sides. I need to look directly at the person I want to dance with and he or she needs to look right back. Then there's the nod (plus maybe a smile or an eyebrow wiggle) and we're off. So we both choose our dancers. This wordless mutual agreement can be quite magical once you get the hang of it. It's like you establish this secret accord that no one else knows about until suddenly you're on the dance floor and in each other's arms, ready for an awesome *tanda*.

Outside the *milonga*

If you want to get really good at tango, you have to make that decision; you have to know you want it and go after it.

Some time ago, I watched an interesting TED talk about what makes successful people successful. The common factor mentioned was "grit," which was likened to perseverance or determination. (You may recall that I listed determination as an ingredient for tango success in the previous lesson.) I was watching the video with my kids' education in mind, but when I look at the top dancers around me, I see that deeper something, that grit. It goes beyond their talent and years invested. It's that drive and determination that amplifies the talent, fuels the hard work, and gives them a deep-seated belief that because they want to get there, they will. And they do. And so can you.

Tango has taught me a lot about decisiveness. I believe I am a better dancer, teacher, and business person because of it. That insecure person is still within me, but alongside her walks a much more confident person who knows what she wants and often goes after it. I live a more fulfilling life because of her.

~ Lesson 16 ~

ACCEPT THAT THINGS WON'T GO ACCORDING TO PLAN

When you feel disappointed and frustrated in life, it's often because something unexpected has happened. For instance, you had your heart set on going to your favourite little Italian restaurant but arrive to find it closed. So you find a Plan B restaurant and one of two things happens:

1. You never really settle in, because it's noisier than the other place or the menu isn't what you were looking forward to all day. Not only do you have trouble enjoying

the meal, the ambience, or even the company—you also feel some nagging resentment toward the other restaurant. It's a stupid night for them to be closed, and they should announce their hours better so this kind of thing doesn't happen to people. Your plans were foiled and your night is more or less ruined.

2. You soak up the energy of the bustling place and decide to try a dish you've never had before. It turns out to be interesting, if not the best thing you've ever tasted. The appetizers and wine are delicious, and you and your friends have fun listening in on the bizarre conversation at the next table. You still plan to visit your intimate little Italian place soon, but now you have a new spot to add to your list. Oh, and you mentally note that you should call ahead and make a reservation next time. It will save you from showing up to a closed door *and* from waiting for a table.

This is an example of how you can experience the exact same events in completely different ways depending on how you perceive and react to them. If you allow resentment over unexpected changes to weigh heavily on you, it will be hard to have a good time no matter what. But if you let go of the initial plan, who knows what can happen?

Dancing in a *milonga* is all about letting go of the plan and adapting to new, unexpected, constantly evolving situations.

Leaders learn this early on, or at least they should. A skilled leader basically has a plan all the time but is expert at instantly changing it. Yes, sometimes the dance floor is overcrowded or downright chaotic. But that is the reality of tango, and if you can't accept that a huge part of dancing a totally improvised dance is learning to react and adjust to what's going on around you, it will be hard to have fun when there are other couples on the dance floor.

With your partner, mistakes will be made. The sooner you can accept this, the more you will enjoy tango. Finding creative ways to get out of a sticky situation can even be a fun challenge. I'm sure half of the new moves that are invented start as accidents. In fact, a good portion of my *adornos* come about while I'm trying to disguise a misstep.

If you've read the other lessons in this book, you know that I really, really don't like it when social dancers "teach" their partners. Leaders who correct their followers on what they were "supposed to" have done are too attached to their initial plan. They're unable to just adapt and move on. It's so much nicer to dance with someone who laughs off the inevitable mistakes and their weird results. The same goes for leaders who are constantly annoyed by all the dancers around them. Why bother with frustration? The beauty of tango lies in its unpredictability. That is what keeps it fresh and new even as we dance around the same floor to the same music over and over again.

I once danced with a man who criticized literally all the dancers around us throughout the entire *tanda*. This one didn't advance enough, that one was too close behind us, people in general should move faster. His complaining made him so unpleasant to dance with that I still remember it years later. But imagine going through life like that, constantly annoyed by and critical of everything that goes on around you? I think it would be hard to get much enjoyment out of anything.

Followers often hold on too tightly to their doubt and insecurity over what their leader's plan might have been. "Was that right?" "Was that what he wanted me to do?" The answer is "It doesn't matter." What's done is done, and it's up to both partners to just take things from there.

That's on the dance floor, but off the dance floor the unexpected can happen as well. Just like in the restaurant example, you may not have the exact night you were looking forward to, but if you're open to what comes, you can still have a great time. Didn't dance as many *tandas* as you hoped? Well, maybe tonight was more about enjoying the vibe than filling your dance card. Didn't catch a *cabeceo* from the person you most wanted to tango with? Maybe you made someone else's night when they did catch *yours*.

Tango has helped me realize that many of life's frustrating moments boil down to the ability to let go of the plan. And that ability is directly linked to living fully in the here and now.

If living in the moment and going with the flow are ideas you already live by, that part of tango may come to you with relative ease (as it did for me back when I started). But if rolling with the punches is difficult for you, perhaps tango will teach you the life lesson of letting go.

~ Lesson 17 ~

BE GOOD TO YOUR FEET

Our feet support our whole bodies. They bear our weight and allow us to stand, walk, run, jump, and, of course, dance. There is barely a move we humans make that doesn't involve those hardworking babies at the ends of our legs. Considering all they do for us, we ought to be thankful to our feet and do right by them.

Tango is particularly tough on our feet. If you use your feet effectively while dancing tango, you exaggerate the rolling-through motion of the foot from heel to toes when you walk forward. This is what allows you to better control your landings and gain maximum propulsion. You've no doubt heard at least one teacher say to "push the floor." When walking, transferring your weight, or pivoting, you need to push into the metatarsals and through the toes to generate powerful movements that your partner will feel. This is an essential part of good tango technique, but it puts a lot of pressure on the balls of the feet. And if, like most people, you have spent much of your life underusing your feet, you may suddenly find yourself with tired, sore, or even injured ones.

Underusing? But didn't I just say we use our feet for almost every movement we make? Interestingly, despite the fact that we constantly move around and load our feet with weight, we generally underuse their intrinsic muscles because we spend so much of our lives wearing shoes and walking around on hard, flat surfaces. We don't work the strength, flexibility, or even mobility of our feet thoroughly, so the muscles atrophy and our feet become weak and prone to pain and injury.

Young children generally have broad soles and splayed toes. They also have better foot dexterity than adults and can do things like wiggle their toes individually. Most of us lose this ability in adulthood, but in barefoot cultures around the world people retain that foot dexterity into old age.

It's also worth nothing that many knee, hip, and back problems begin with the feet. The good news is that most foot problems are biomechanical, meaning they're caused by the way we stand, the way we move, or the shoes we wear. Why is that good? Because it means biomechanics can resolve the problem as well.

Some things you can do to take care of your feet

Check your foot position. How do you place your feet when you stand and walk? How do you place your feet when you stand and walk? If you are standing, your feet should be parallel with each other, with the toes facing forward rather than turned in or out. In tango, we generally recommend keeping a slight "V" shape between the feet, so your heels are together and the fronts of your feet are slightly outward-facing. The degree, however, should be very small – this will help stabilize you without messing with your joint alignment. Also, you should have equal pressure on the inner and outer edges of the feet, so you are neither pronating (rolling in) nor supinating (rolling out) when you stand or walk. (To clarify, I am talking about the weight-bearing leg here. In tango, we do allow the free ankle to pronate, or roll in, but not the standing one.) When in motion it is important to mobilize your feet and ankles and to pay attention to the rolling-through process of each step, forward and backward. Also, your toes should not be jammed into the floor. Your centre of gravity should be carried far enough back that your toes are free to lift and wiggle, and that centre should stay back even when you are in motion. This all brings me to my next point.

Maintain correct postural alignment. This refers to how the head, shoulders, spine, hips, knees, and ankles line up with each other. Proper alignment of the body helps you achieve and maintain good posture, and it will improve your dancing. Poor alignment puts stress on the spine and other articulations and can ultimately cause joint degeneration. For more about posture and alignment, read Lesson 8.

I'll wrap up this section with a note about my personal experience:

It was through yoga more than anything that I began to really grasp proper alignment and how to stand correctly. When I was younger, I couldn't fathom why I could run 10 kilometres or dance all night with relative ease but couldn't stand for more than 20 minutes without extreme fatigue and soreness in my feet. I eventually learned that I was carrying my centre of gravity too far forward, which put a lot of stress on my metatarsal joints (and a lot of weight on my tango partners). Whether standing, walking, or dancing tango, our axis should be carried over our heels. The heel bone is the largest bone in the foot, and it's made to support our body weight. Now that I know how to properly align myself, I can stand for much longer periods of time without pain or fatigue. Even my high heels tire my feet less. But that doesn't mean I wear them more, which brings me to my next point.

Choose your shoes with care. For *tangueros,* the main question is: "Why dance shoes and not just comfy street shoes?" Because dance shoes have a good balance of support and flexibility, they fit the shape of your foot well, and the soles are neither very thick nor wider than the upper part of the shoe (so you can get a good feel for the floor, your partner's feet, and the movements of your own feet). Just be sure to get a good fit with enough width for your toes.

For *tangueras,* it's a whole other story. Most women's tango shoes have high heels. Very high heels. Very high stiletto heels. I think everyone knows that high heels are not good for us. Countless articles and books have been written on this topic, and studies show again and again that long-term wearing of high heels harms women's bodies. It affects our feet, our knees, our hips, our backs, and even our leg muscles.

There seems to be little consensus on what the ideal heel height should be for healthy feet. Some experts say the optimal height is 1 to 1.5 inches (2.5 to 4 centimetres); others say it's a totally flat heel. Still others say it varies from person to person based on the shape of their feet. Yet no one seems to recommend 3.5-inch (9-centimetre) stilettos as optimal footwear.

I've been wearing heels to dance tango for more than 20 years. For the first 10, I didn't feel many ill effects aside from sore feet at the end of a long night of dancing and permanent calluses (the so-called dancer's pad) under the middles of the balls of my feet. But since I opened my school and made tango my full-time job, my feet have felt it. It's not just the shoes, of course. It's partly the sheer number of hours I spend on my feet. (I dance five or six days a week and can spend up to nine hours a day teaching, practising, and dancing.) And I don't wear heels all the time; I probably don't wear them even half the time. The older I get and the more I study posture, alignment, and biomechanics, the less often I wear high heels.

So what's a fashion-loving *tanguera* to do? The safest choice for the long-term health of your feet and joints is to give up the high heels and dance in low-heeled shoes or flats instead. "But they just don't look or feel the same as dancing in sexy heels!" It's true. If, like me, you're not yet ready to give up the sexy shoes altogether, I suggest the following:

- Vary your dance footwear and your heel heights. Change your shoes often—about every two hours if you'll be on your feet longer than that. Make sure you have at least one pair of low-heeled practice shoes in your collection.

- As much as possible, save the high heels for the *milongas*. Spend most of your class and practice time in lower-heeled shoes, and don't wear high heels at all outside of tango. Everything in life is about balance. A few hours a week in high heels probably won't do you much harm if you're wearing sensible shoes the rest of the time. (Also, avoid spending a lot of time in flip-flops. They're terrible for your feet, too.)
- Make sure that the high-heeled shoes you do wear fit your feet well. Make especially sure that they're wide enough for you. Thankfully, those closed-toe pointy things are no longer in fashion. The sandal-style shoes all the *tangueras* wear these days at least allow the toes some space to move and spread a little.
- Train your body to stay properly aligned, even in your tango shoes. Hips over heels, always. To facilitate this, the heel of your shoe should be placed right under the heel of your foot (not too far back) and should feel stable.
- Regularly exercise your feet and stretch your legs. Focus especially on your calves, which get shortened by repeated wearing of high heels. But don't forget your hamstrings, either. (Yoga, anyone?) Read on for specific foot exercises.

Exercise your feet to improve their strength, flexibility, and mobility.

- Do toe workouts, including lifting your toes up while standing, spreading your toes, and moving each toe individually. Many people cannot really do this last one, but with practice you can retrain the necessary little muscles and eventually see results. (I've been working on toe agility for a few years now and have made significant progress. I'm sure it's good for my brain as well!) If you have a deviated big toe due to hallux valgus or bunions, these exercises can help you realign it with the inner line of the foot, improving your condition. Such exercises can also help prevent these conditions from developing in the first place.

- Do exercises to both strengthen and stretch the soles and arches of the feet. Strengthening exercises include scrunching up a towel using your toes, picking up marbles or other small objects using your toes, and scrunching up your toes without any props. Here's a good stretch exercise for the feet: Kneel on the floor (with a folded towel under your knees), sitting on your heels with your toes extended (tucked under). Hold for 30 seconds or as long as you can bear it.

- Massage the soles of your feet with a tennis ball. Doing this while standing is best because you can put a good amount of pressure on the different parts of your feet. If your feet are too sensitive at first, you can do it while sitting in a chair. This massage eventually feels great, and it somewhat mimics walking barefoot on uneven surfaces—something our ancient ancestors did that few of us do today.

- Elevate your feet. This is a great thing to do anytime, really, but especially after a long night of tango dancing. Lie on the floor with your calves resting on the seat of a chair or your legs straight up against a wall. Elevating your legs will improve your circulation as it reduces foot and leg fatigue or swelling.

- Pamper those hardworking babies. Soak sore feet in warm or cold water. Massage them with a soothing foot lotion before bed. Treat yourself to a foot massage or pedicure.

• Walk barefoot on the beach. Great for the soles, great for the soul.

If you have foot pain that is acute or long-lasting, see a professional. My specialist of choice is an excellent physiotherapist who has helped me through many minor injuries over the years. You might prefer a podiatrist, osteopath, or other specialist, but if you're in pain, get it looked into. Did you know that 25 percent of our bones are in the feet and ankles? Not to mention the 33 joints and more than 100 muscles, tendons, and ligaments found in the feet. That's a lot of little parts that can get injured.

My partner and I have had our share of foot ailments: hallux valgus, metatarsalgia, plantar fasciitis, stress fractures, and an enchondroma. I also have tight, overdeveloped calves, which limit my flexibility and mobility. Whether this is a result of all that ballet in my teen years, all the high heels in my tango years, simple genetics, or a combination of all three, I don't know—but I make a point of stretching my calf muscles almost every day now.

I beat up my feet with my lifestyle, but more and more I make sure to set aside a little time each day to take care of them, too. That way, they can keep taking care of me and my dancing for many years to come.

~ Lesson 18 ~

THE CODES OF CONDUCT EXIST
FOR GOOD REASON

We're all (hopefully) familiar with the universal rules of courtesy and good manners. But there are codes that apply specifically to social dancing and even more specifically to Argentine tango.

I believe more firmly in tango's *códigos* (codes of conduct) every day, and I reinforce them in my teaching. These rules of etiquette are not meant to limit or restrict people's freedom or enjoyment. On the contrary, they exist to ensure that a pleasurable time can be had by all.

I hope this lesson will serve as both a guide for beginners going to their first *milongas* and a friendly reminder for those who have been dancing a while.

Off the dance floor

Crossing the dance floor. When you enter a *milonga* or need to cross from one side of the dance floor to the other, always go around the floor, not through the middle.

The *mirada-cabeceo* invitation system. As I mentioned before (see Lesson 15), I'm an increasingly strong supporter of the *mirada-cabeceo* invitation system. Let's recap exactly what this is:

Mirada means "look," *cabeceo* means "nod," and together they make up the traditional, non-verbal, and most widely accepted way of inviting and getting invited to dance tango. Basically, leader and follower look directly at the person they wish to dance with and, hopefully, catch each other's eye. Then the leader nods or motions with his or her head and the follower nods or smiles his or her acceptance.

It's worth practising it because it works.

Followers aren't stuck waiting around for an invitation. This can be especially empowering for female followers. Incredibly, there are still people out there who frown upon women doing the inviting, but with the *cabeceo,* the line between inviter and invitee is blurred. After all, if I want to dance with him, I'm the one who has to look him in the eye . . . then he nods and I smile, or was it me who nodded and him who smiled?

As a leader, you're not asking directly and risking outright rejection or a reluctant "yes" from someone who doesn't really want to dance with you but doesn't want to hurt your feelings.

For both leaders and followers, to accept or not to accept becomes a non-issue. Because you have to make eye contact to invite or be invited, if you don't want to dance with someone, you just don't make eye contact. No need to refuse or make up excuses. Each dance is a mutual agreement. You both actively choose each other. This subtle assertiveness may not always be easy for shy types, but if you master the technique, who knows? You may actually overcome some of your shyness at the same time.

Of course, nothing is foolproof. The one drawback here is the risk of confusion. If the room is large, dark, or crowded, it can be hard to tell who is looking at whom, so when someone nods toward your table, it may be difficult to discern the target. If you nod at someone and the wrong person accepts, the kind and polite thing to do is to dance the *tanda* with your unintended and hope you're more on target next time.

In any case, this should all take place after the *tanda* starts and not during the *cortina* (though feel free to scan the room, plan ahead, and be ready). Why? Because you're supposed to choose your dancers and the music in relation to one another. In my case, there are some dancers I prefer for quick, rhythmic *milongas*. I save most waltzes for a few specific partners and dramatic Puglieses for others. Sure, there are dancers I will happily dance anything with—my own partner, for one—but they are the exception. Connection is just as much about the music as the person in your arms, and when the two fit well together, it can be magical.

The verbal invitation. While I encourage use of the *cabeceo*, there are instances in which it's just fine to verbally invite someone. If you happen to be standing right next to a person you want to dance with, it makes sense to use words. If you're having a conversation with someone and a great *tanda* starts up, of course you would ask the person verbally.

Whom to dance with. As advanced dancers, we should accept at least a few invitations regardless of the inviter's skill level. It's one way we can help beginners to improve their dancing. Meanwhile, if we reject based on bad behaviour, we may help some dancers to work on that. I generally don't avoid or refuse people based on skill level; I make my decisions based on attitude and dance-floor etiquette.

Leaders I avoid are those who push, pull, and generally manhandle me so much that I have to spend every second fighting for my balance. I also try to steer clear of those who show a complete disregard for the other dancers on the floor. Dancing with leaders who use their partners like shields or weapons is really stressful; followers end up looking over their shoulders and trying to do the leader's job of avoiding collisions. Also high on my "avoid" list are dancers who correct or teach their partners on the dance floor.

What do I look for when I'm considering whether to accept an invitation? Connection to me; attention to dance-floor flow and safety; musicality. Creative figures and fun moves are on the list, but not if they get in the way of the aforementioned items.

Cutting in. Nope. Not during a song, not in between songs. It's not even good manners to grab someone who's still on the dance floor during the *cortina*. You just aren't supposed to invite someone who's already on the dance floor.

Entering the dance floor. Please don't forget this second, equally important use of the *cabeceo*. When entering the line of dance with your partner, you must be conscious of oncoming traffic and avoid cutting right in front of an approaching couple. Unless you can easily merge, leaving several paces free in front of the next couple, make eye contact with the leader before you merge and wait for their acknowledgement. When you're dancing, be aware of the dance floor's entry points and allow other couples to merge as needed. This avoids unfortunate collisions and establishes mutual respect among the leaders on the floor.

On the dance floor

The *tanda*. *Tandas* are sets of three or four songs by one orchestra or of a similar style. *Tandas* are separated by *cortinas,* which are short clips of non-tango music. Normally, we are meant to finish a full *tanda* with the same partner. Being left partway through a set feels bad. So barring exceptional circumstances, remember that a *tanda* lasts but 9 to 12 minutes of your life. Even if it's unpleasant, you can probably grin and bear it. However, there are three instances in which it is acceptable to stop dancing partway through a set:

- Both partners came to a mutual agreement before the dance began.
- An injury or other emergency occurs during the dance.
- A partner's behaviour is so rude or disrespectful that it merits offending or embarrassing them by abandoning them mid-*tanda.*

Respect the *ronda*. Leaders, follow the *ronda,* or line of dance. This means not weaving randomly from one line (lane) to another and not speeding around the floor cutting in front of all the other couples. Ideally, leaders should maintain an equal distance from the couple ahead throughout the song. Also ideally, every couple should finish each song positioned ahead of and behind the same couple they started out ahead of and behind. To avoid collisions, leaders should always look ahead rather than down. To this same end, they should also back up infrequently and with care. Respecting the *ronda* is probably one of the most difficult parts of learning to lead, but I think it's a little less difficult if you adjust your perspective: Instead of seeing the other couples on the floor simply as obstacles to be avoided, see them as an integral part of your dancing. We should dance *with* the other couples, not *against* or *despite* them. Imagine the whole dance floor moving as one, each couple unique but everyone together. What a flow there would be.

Followers, stay within the space your partner creates for you and avoid kicking up your feet unless you're sure it's safe. This means that if you dance with your eyes closed, you really shouldn't ever be kicking your feet up behind you. Meanwhile, if your eyes are open, it's okay to physically stop your partner from taking that step backward if it means avoiding a collision.

Less talk, more dancing. One more time: Please avoid teaching or correcting your partner. Dance to his or her level, and when something isn't working, try to improve *your own* technique. Corrections are the job of teachers and should be saved for class time. In general, postpone the conversation until the music stops. Constant apologies for every misstep are almost as distracting as corrections. And if you want to chat about the weather or discuss your day, have a seat at the bar.

Quality, not quantity. It's the connection that counts. Limit your large movements, especially when the dance floor is full. And, once again, don't lead or execute any off-the-floor *boleos* without first ensuring you have plenty of room to do so.

It's been said that the *tanguero* who dances non-stop for three hours straight doesn't really love tango—he just needs to keep moving. Supposedly, a "real" dancer chooses his music and his partners discerningly, and one is often a consequence of the other. I think there's definitely room for both types of dancer in every *milonga*, but try not to get discouraged or bitter if you didn't get as many *tandas* as you hoped. Some nights are like that, and one great *tanda* is sometimes enough to make your evening.

No hit and runs! Accidents happen. Never mind whose fault it was; it's just good manners to say sorry, make sure the other person is okay—and be more careful next time.

About hygiene

It's important to shower, brush your teeth, and put on deodorant before heading to tango class or the *milonga*. Yes, I kind of hate that I even have to tell people this. But there are still some who either don't know or don't care that stale breath and other body odours are unpleasant to others—never mind that they might very well make the difference between a *mirada* and an averted gaze.

What I hate even more is having to tell people to wash their hands after using the toilet, but I know for a fact there are women and men who don't; I have seen it with my own eyes. Right now, as the COVID-19 pandemic continues to spread across the planet, handwashing and hand sanitizing are obviously all the rage. But clean hands prevent the spread of all kinds of infection and disease, not just coronaviruses. One day, hopefully in the not-too-distant future, we'll once again hold live social tango events. When that time comes, we will remind you to wash or sanitize after using the bathrooms—and as you enter and exit the premises and in between tandas. And we will insist you stay home if you have cold or flu symptoms. We might all be wearing masks for the first months back as well. But even when this crisis becomes a thing of the past, I hope we'll all remember to wash our hands often for the safety of all—and to freshen up regularly for the comfort of all.

So those are the "rules" of Argentine tango. They're a lot to take in at first. But with practice, the codes and customs will become as integral a part of your dancing as walking, embracing your partner, and following the rhythm. After all, when you learn to drive a car, operating the vehicle is just a small part of the package. You also have to follow the flow of traffic, avoid collisions, and be aware and respectful of everyone else on the road. Shouldn't it be the same on the dance floor?

~ Lesson 19 ~

PRACTISE KINDNESS

Lesson 6 ("It's nice to be important, but it's more important to be nice") is by far the most popular post on my blog. Which indicates that some people don't necessarily perceive their fellow tango dancers as the most sympathetic bunch.

Revisiting this topic, I feel the need to make a distinction between being "nice" and being "kind."

Those who are overly concerned with being nice are often motivated by the need for approval from other people. They might even overlook their own wellbeing to accommodate others.

The motivation to be kind, however, is more internal. People who aim for kindness are less concerned about what others might think and more interested in doing the right thing. Their respect for others is balanced by their own self-respect.

In tango, "nice" people accept dances with anyone and everyone because they don't want to hurt people's feelings or be perceived as rude or snobby. It's a good thing not to want to hurt someone, but if your previous experience with a person was highly unpleasant, you should not feel obligated to repeat it to your own detriment.

"Kind" dancers, on the other hand, might reserve a few *tandas* for hardworking dancers of a lower level and the lonely newcomer who hasn't danced all night, but they still know when to say no.

I used to be an overly "nice" person—in life and in dance—so I sometimes let people walk all over me. I felt guilty every time I had to say no to someone. This sort of personality doesn't work so well in either parenting or business, so as I grew up, I learned that I can still be a kind person without necessarily always being nice.

If you want to be truly kind in tango, I believe you need to occasionally dance with beginners. That being said, it's important to point out what several readers have mentioned in comments on my blog posts: A beginner is not the same as a bad dancer who has not attempted to improve in a decade. If I know someone still takes classes and works hard, I'm happy to dance with them regardless of their current level. However, if they think they're really good simply because they've been dancing for 15 years? If they still zigzag all over the dance floor and correct their partners when they don't execute a move as intended? They will receive my polite refusal.

I believe that teaching should be done through encouragement and positive reinforcement. That means I tell students what they're doing wrong *and* what they're doing right. For me, that second part comes easiest. Early on, it was actually hard for me to point out people's misalignments and postural flaws, especially when they were blatantly unaware and it meant I had to burst their bubble. But students come to me to learn and most of them appreciate a little candour. I've discovered that in general people have a thicker skin than I thought. In any case, a good teacher can make students aware of what they're doing wrong and what needs to be improved without diminishing or criticizing them in a negative or hurtful way.

As I said in the previous lesson, I firmly believe that following the *códigos* of the *milonga* is important and will ultimately improve everyone's experience. I also believe that injecting our *milonga*-going selves with some generosity will go a long way toward the greater good. And the two are not mutually exclusive. For example, I fully support the use of the *cabeceo,* but I don't reject invitations on principle just because they were made verbally. If I'm happy to dance with you, I'll accept your invitation, silent or verbal, as long as it is respectful.

On the dance floor, the nicest dancers to tango with are those who let go of their egos and dance with generosity. Skill level plays a part, of course, but with or without stellar technique, if your partner makes you feel he or she is taking care of you, you will feel pretty good.

Here's how you can take care of your partners:

- Dance to their level, thus making them feel good about their dancing. Do this instead of concerning yourself with showing off all your best moves or *adornos*.
- Do everything in your power to avoid collisions. If an accident does happen, make sure no one is hurt and apologize to all concerned; don't get defensive and look to place blame.
- Ignore or laugh off any mistakes or miscommunications. Accept that errors are part of tango. Whatever you do, do not instruct, correct, or otherwise comment on your partners' dancing when things don't go as planned.

If you and your partners follow these guidelines, you will all feel safe, connected, and at ease. You might even find that you don't want a particular *tanda* to end—and you will certainly seek out another one later.

Be kind and you will ultimately contribute to the growth and improvement of others, yourself, and the community as a whole.

~ Lesson 20 ~

WORK HARD, HAVE FUN

It happens somewhere between the beginner and intermediate phases: Many (if not most) tango students realize that this fun social dance is more work than they anticipated.

This revelation affects people differently.

Some drop out. They decide that the hours of practice every week and the regular blows to the ego in the form of corrections and adjustments by teachers are too much. Tango isn't the fun date-night activity they had in mind.

Others keep going but stop advancing. They have enough moves and partners to enjoy themselves at *milongas*, so why kill the buzz with hard and boring stuff like posture and—yuck—technique? They're content where they are and don't feel driven to take things further.

Then there are those who are fuelled by the challenge of this simple yet complex dance. They work ever harder, feeling rewarded every time they overcome a hurdle—only to be faced with the next. For these dancers, the hard work isn't just a means to an end; it is itself a huge part of the enjoyment.

The cool thing is that the harder you work, the easier it gets. As you improve your posture, strengthen your legs, and develop your tango communication skills, the physical and mental effort of dancing and all the multi-tasking it requires decreases. So if you're feeling like you might quit sometime soon, I suggest reading on and giving it at least one more shot. You can still have fun while working hard to improve your dancing. Here's how.

Focus on the important stuff

Almost all beginner dancers are impressed by the fancy moves they see in shows and on YouTube. Many dancers put pressure on themselves (and their partners) to learn lots and lots of these cool moves and to execute as many of them as possible in as short a time as possible. Your teachers might tell you that the moves are not the important thing, but this is not easy to believe at first. After all, it's difficult to grasp the importance of a caring and comfortable embrace, musical precision, and a mastery of floorcraft when you haven't yet felt the pleasure that can be derived from those things. What can I say besides this: "Believe us!" Yes, you need some vocabulary, but you don't need to use all your vocabulary all the time. Imagine a comfortable and sincere embrace, precise and playful musicality, a smooth dance-floor flow, and a few simple moves executed well. Now imagine trying to remember and execute all the crazy moves and *adornos* you have seen in your entire tango life. Which sounds better? Which sounds more stressful?

Believe that hard work truly is its own reward

The process of learning and practising doesn't have to be a means to an end. There is a lot of satisfaction to be gained from the simple act of making an effort. Nowhere is this more true than in an activity like tango. But there will be so many other rewards that automatically stem from the work, such as becoming an increasingly sought-after tango partner, improving brain function (as more and more studies tell us), and keeping good posture and joint mobility throughout life.

Concentrate more on self-improvement than what everyone else is doing wrong

Focus on your partner's shortcomings and you will find more and more of them, guaranteed. This will lead to frustration and impatience on both sides. But focus on what you can do to make your partner comfortable and the dance will run more smoothly, even if your partner really isn't very good. Feel annoyed every time another couple cuts it a little too close and you will spend a lot of your floor time peeved. Come up with a few fun go-to solutions to these inevitable realities and you can practically turn the whole thing into a game.

Remember that you cannot control events; you can only control how you react to them. On the tango dance floor, this means you can neither control how your partner reacts nor how the couples around you react—but you *can* control how you handle your side of the equation. So when things aren't going according to plan, resist the urge to make impatient sounds or to correct your partner. Instead, examine and work on your own skills: Stand straighter, drop your shoulders, fully connect your legs in between steps, listen more, slow down. You'll have worked to improve yourself, you'll have given your partner a more pleasurable experience, and you'll have made yourself a more desirable dancer in the process.

Remember that others are not to blame for your bad nights

Sometimes you'll have a bad night, no matter who you are. Maybe at last week's lesson you finally felt you were moving up the learning curve, yet tonight you hit not just a plateau but a wall. Perhaps you arrived at the *milonga* dressed to the nines and ready to dance the night away, but you only got two *tandas* in and both felt substandard. Hard as it is, the best thing to do is accept that yes, you had a disappointing night—then move on. Don't wallow in it, blame your inadequate partner, resent your teacher or the *milonga* organizer, or hold a grudge against all the dancers who didn't invite you. And maybe don't vent all over Facebook, either. Feel how you feel, accept both the events and your thoughts about them, then do whatever you can to let it all go. And don't let one bad night (or even two or three) crush you. Instead, use it to drive you further along that learning curve. Sign up for a private lesson, ask a teacher or admired dancer for advice, arrange to practise with a friend, make an agreement with your partner to be less critical of each other in class.

So that's my advice on how to work hard and play hard. I live this balance every day. Yes, I work hard. Really, really hard. Many people do, and anyone who runs a small, hands-on business does. The work sometimes overwhelms me and there are days that get me down. I worry about my overworked feet and back, get frustrated with my own dancing, butt heads with my partner, face unfriendly competition, cringe at my bank balance ... But the rewards! I am constantly surrounded by movement and music and wonderful people. I dance and teach and host parties and create playlists of my favourite music every single week. So I also have fun. So much fun. Not despite the fact that I work really, really hard but *because* of it.

So work hard to have fun and have fun working hard.

~ Lesson 21 ~

TANGO IS NOT FOR EVERYONE

In more than two decades of dancing, 20 years of teaching, and 13 years running my own studio, I have seen more people drop out of tango than stick with it.

On my school's website, I state that tango *is* for everyone and that "If you can walk, you can dance." I stand by those statements: You can take up tango whether you're 25 or 65, male or female, single or in a couple, shy or extroverted—the list goes on. But just because you can walk doesn't mean you will dance tango like a pro. It also doesn't mean you will love tango. And to keep dancing tango, you've got to love it. Because while the concept is simple, the dance is not so easy.

As a tango-lover and tango teacher, I think it would be great if everyone at least gave tango a try. You might like it, love it, stick with it, and get really good at it. Or you might not.

Let's look at some reasons why tango might not be for you.

You only stick with things that come easy

Beginners soon realize that if they're going to dance this dance, they will have to dedicate a significant amount of time to it. One class a week is not sufficient, and you're probably not going to feel like you're really dancing in less than a year.

You won't stick with tango beyond a few weeks of classes if you don't develop a desire to really work on your dancing, which means working on yourself.

Tango, as all experienced dancers know, is about much more than memorizing a few steps or sequences. It is about connection and communication, posture and a smooth walk, musicality and improvisation. And those things take *years* to develop and—maybe, just maybe—master.

If all this sounds unpleasantly daunting to you, maybe you're on the wrong track. If it sounds more like an exciting challenge, keep going.

You expect tango to be just another series of dance steps

If you're coming to tango from other social dances—ballroom or Latin, for example—don't expect to skip the beginner levels because of your experience. Every dance is different, Argentine tango is unique, and you sure aren't going to pick it up in some kind of 10-dances-in-10-weeks format.

In Lesson 2, I compared learning tango to learning a new language. If you speak multiple languages already, you might pick new ones up more easily—but speaking English and Italian doesn't mean you can skip to advanced-level Russian. Similarly, past dance experience might help you learn tango faster: You may have developed your body awareness, sense of rhythm, and lead/follow skills. But you still need to learn the basics. And you might also have to unlearn some of your other dance technique—turned-out knees, loose hips, or lifted elbows, for example.

Learning tango is about developing technique as you integrate a whole new vocabulary into your body. The steps and sequences are but a small part of what it's all about. It is the discovery of a world all its own and like no other. If you're ready and willing make this discovery, you're heading down the right path.

You have very fragile self-esteem

I previously said that you need a thick skin to dance tango. If your self-esteem is in a fragile state, tango may not be the boost you need right now.

Take up tango and you will discover that you have to relearn how to walk, your posture needs work, and you don't really know how to embrace someone. Tango will probably break you down before it builds you up.

And then there is the social aspect. Everyone has bad nights when we don't get the dances we hoped for. It can be a struggle not to let such a night leave us feeling deflated, undesirable, or resentful.

Some of us are crushed by these kinds of challenges, but some are inspired by and driven to overcome them.

Tango is your romanticized idea of a date-night activity with your sweetheart

A session of tango lessons seems like a great way to inject a little extra passion into your relationship, right? And I'm not saying that it's not. But people conjure up these rose-filled clichés about tango—that it's all passion and sexiness and that it will magically bring those things into their lives and their relationship.

Okay, eventually it might. But not in the ways you imagine and not without you putting in some serious time, dedication, and hard work in the process.

I hate to admit it, but tango can actually be quite hard on a couple (more on that in the next lesson). The whole partnering thing can be complicated in so many ways, whether you take up tango on your own or with your significant other.

To make a long story short, learning tango together will take patience, understanding, a sense of humour, and a good dose of humility on both sides. But if you're able to work on all these things, not only will it be fun and romantic—it might even make your relationship stronger.

You're signing up for tango lessons in the hopes of meeting a mate

It happens. I met my partner through tango; my brother met his wife through tango. But in both cases, it was years in. If you're going to stick with tango long enough to get good at it, you need to love the dance enough to spend a lot of time and effort working on it. Sure, you *might* meet that special someone through tango. Accept it if it happens, but don't expect it to happen. Speed dating, tango is not.

When my school offers free trial classes for newcomers, we can immediately spot the ones who are there with an ulterior motive. They rarely last long; the dance will just take too much work if dating is the real goal.

Of course, it takes all kinds to make a (tango) world, so there are a few long-time dancers in every community who both love the dance itself *and* use it to get up close and personal with those they see as potential mates.

All that said, if you're signing up for tango lessons as a way to meet *people,* it might be among the best things you can do. You will encounter all kinds of fascinating folks at tango classes and tango events, all of whom have a significant common interest. More than a couple activity, tango is a social activity, so you will most certainly make friends and become part of a whole new circle.

You really don't have room in your life for an all-consuming pursuit

If you want to dance tango, you have to let tango in. Once a week is not enough. Twice a week is not even enough. And if you grow to love this dance, three, four, five times a week may not feel like enough. Tango has a tendency to take over people's lives, at least for a time. It almost has to if you're going to get good at it. Tango is often referred to as an obsession, an addiction, a drug. Tango dancers live, breathe, and consume their passion. If you take up this dance in a serious way, you are letting it into your life. This will affect your calendar, your bank balance, your social life, and your soul.

If you're not afraid of a few years of hard work and the occasional humbling experience, tango may be for you. If you want to make new friends and discover something challenging, profound, and potentially revealing about yourself or your relationship, tango may be for you. Or tango may not be for you. You won't know for sure unless you give it a try and see where it leads.

~ Lesson 22 ~

TANGO IS HARD ON COUPLES

When you say "tango," people conjure up images of roses, romance, and passion. Tango lessons certainly do seem like a great couples activity, so it can be surprising when you sign up for classes and find awkwardness, frustration, defensiveness, or jealousy instead. If this sounds familiar, you are not alone.

Over our years in tango together, my partner and I have seen just about every issue a couple can face—and we even experienced some ourselves early on. There are many possible scenarios, each with its own challenges. Just understand this: Tango does not cause relationship issues, but it can amplify existing ones.

Some friends and I were talking about this phenomenon a while ago and we came up with a slogan: "If your relationship can survive tango, your relationship can survive anything!" While I won't be making this my school's new motto, there is a significant element of truth to it.

I'll present some common situations and the issues that can arise from them. We'll also look at possible solutions that will increase the chance of your relationship surviving tango—and of tango surviving your relationship.

You take up tango together

In a group class, it's typical for beginners to dance with beginners. This is never easy, however. A beginner-leading-beginner situation can amplify relationship issues such as defensiveness, impatience, and jealousy.

Defensiveness. To learn tango—to learn anything—you need to be receptive. If you're defensive every time the teacher corrects you or your partner doesn't respond as you hoped, you will block your own capacity to learn while placing most or all of the blame on your partner.

Keep in mind that we tend to be less tolerant toward those we feel comfortable with, so when your tango partner is also your life partner, you might blame him or her for missteps more readily than you would a stranger. Spending a lot of time trying to figure out who is to blame is unproductive. Work as a team (with the help of your teachers) and you will see that you and your partner both possess solutions.

Impatience. Remember, you and your partner will probably not pick up the dance at exactly the same pace. Either partner might be a quicker study, and if that partner is you, you're going to have to be extra patient with your partner. If your partner is the faster learner, you're going to have to be extra patient with yourself.

As I mentioned in Lesson 12, the early stages of the learning curve are often hardest for leaders. This is why they receive the brunt of the impatience and frustration—from both parties. Followers with a touch of natural skill can feel they dance well pretty quickly if paired with an experienced leader. But for leaders, there is a lot to think about and understand right from the start. So both partners might feel—somewhat mistakenly—that the follower is learning faster or dancing better than her partner. Reality sets in later for followers, once they understand there should be so much more to their role than "just following." All of this is normal, but try to remember to be patient and generous toward your partner. You're both probably trying your best.

Jealousy. You may feel insecure when you suddenly see your partner in the arms of somebody else. I've had more than one student come to me and say they just couldn't bear to watch their cherished one clearly having the time of his or her life in another person's embrace. It takes a while to understand that it really is all about the dance and nothing more, that the intensity, connection, and abandon don't leave the dance floor.

If someone is looking for more than the dance, it has nothing to do with tango; tango just may be the chosen avenue. If your life partnership is strong and you trust your partner, tango won't be a problem. If your relationship is fragile and you don't trust your partner, tango may be a dangerous game to play, but it is not to blame.

In my opinion, partner changes are an excellent and necessary tool for improving your dance skills. But they can make novices extremely uncomfortable. This is normal, and in our classes we do not insist people change partners if they're really against the idea. However, if you remain forever unwilling to dance with anyone else—or to allow your mate to—you may not have a future in tango together. Remember, it's just tango. Whether things go well or badly with another partner, you will bring some of what you learned back to your regular partnership.

Learning tango with your mate will take patience, understanding, humility, and—let's not forget—a sense of humour on both sides.

One of you already dances and introduces the other to tango

While beginners leading beginners can be a struggle, experience paired with inexperience presents its own challenges. All kinds of imbalances and issues can come up, including impatience (again), jealousy (again), and inferiority/superiority complexes.

If you have less experience than your partner. Do not put your partner on a pedestal. I see this happen all the time. Sure, if your partner has been dancing for a year and you just started yesterday, he or she will seem like a great dancer to you. But so will almost everyone. And what you need to know is this: A year is nothing in tango. Your partner surely has loads to work on still in terms of his or her technique. So try to focus on learning at your pace without comparing yourself to your partner or getting impatient with yourself. Easier said than done, I know, but idolizing your partner as a dancer will get you nowhere.

If you have more experience than your partner. Do not be condescending. No partnership is truly equal (though the best ones eventually come close), so amplifying the inequalities by constantly finding ways to point them out is counterproductive and will only serve to put your partner on the defensive. And remember that you, too, still have much to learn; you're simply at a different place on the curve. As a teacher, I see condescension manifest itself in two main forms: overly encouraging attitudes and teachy behaviour.

Overly encouraging? Oh yes. Being encouraging is a good thing in principle, but there is a fine line between super supportive and cloyingly condescending. Figuratively patting your partner on the head every single time he or she gets the littlest thing right is almost as annoying as criticizing every imperfection. So give praise when you have a great dance or see real improvement, but make sure it's sincere and doesn't come from too high and mighty a place.

Now, here I go again: Do. Not. Correct. Your. Partner. You may have more experience, but that does not make you a qualified teacher. Be the competent dance partner you know how to be and leave the teaching to the actual teachers. Let your partner learn at his or her pace. And avoid the temptation to constantly show off how much more you know. Nobody likes a know-it-all, unsolicited advice quickly gets irritating, and constantly putting yourself above your lowly partner will probably do little to make him or her feel comfortable.

Also, if *you* are too comfortable in your superior place, watch out: Having more advanced dance skills than your partner is temporary. There's a reasonably good chance that a year or two from now your partner's skills will have caught up to or even surpassed yours—especially if he or she keeps working hard while you remain in your haughty comfort zone.

You both already dance tango when you get together

You basically have two choices here: Agree to make your dancing exclusive or agree to keep dancing with other people. The key word is "agree." Whatever you decide, you both have to be on board, you both have to stick to it, and you both have to allow your partner the same freedoms you expect yourself.

Personally, I would find it difficult to go from dancing with different partners and friends to suddenly shunning them all in order to dance every *tanda* with the same partner—even if that partner was the person I love. This decision would not work for me.

If you choose to dance with others, you will occasionally face the same kind of jealousy that newcomer couples face. It doesn't matter how long you've been dancing or how well you both know that tango is about the dancing. There will be times when you feel your partner has had one *tanda* too many with a particular person or looked a little too blissful in the arms of a certain someone else. I know this because I have lived it, too. Because tango is a full-time job for us, my partner and I had no choice but to get over any emotional insecurities early on. And we fully understand and value the benefits that changing partners brings to our dancing.

So how can you find a mutually agreeable solution to the question of dancing with others? I suggest keeping the lines of communication open and, if necessary, establishing some ground rules. For example, I know some couples who always save the first and/or last *tanda* for each other. It's something special that belongs only to them, but it allows them to keep exploring. They can enjoy other partners, expand their skills, and bring back new experiences to nourish their relationship.

You dance but your mate doesn't

You know as well as I do that tango isn't just another social activity. But then again, it is. If you're going to keep dancing and your mate is not, your mate has to accept that you have an important pastime that doesn't involve them. But this would be true of any activity you're passionate about that you dedicate significant time to, whether it's working out at the gym, singing in a choir, or playing golf. Even if you don't play golf cheek to cheek and chest to chest with your fellow golfers.

To an outsider, this may sound like a rationalization, but it's not: When you're dancing with someone, you're not really dancing with the person; you're dancing with the *dancer*. You can connect—intensely, profoundly, passionately—with a stranger because most of the things about that person don't matter on the dance floor. It doesn't matter what language he speaks, what he does for a living, whether she has children, what her plans are for tomorrow. What matters is the feel of their embrace, their connection to the music, their ability to express, to listen, to follow. Overall, what matters is quite simply what is happening *now*. Tango is a shared moment—well, a shared 10 minutes—and nothing else exists during that moment. This is true whether you're dancing with your life partner or a total stranger. Then the *tanda* is over and you move on to the next connection. These connections are not sexual, but at their best they are quite intimate and profound. You are connecting with something that goes beyond the person in your arms, which is why many of us can derive pleasure from dancing with any gender, regardless of our sexual orientation.

It's possible to confuse these feelings, of course. Sometimes people take (or desire to take) things beyond the dance floor. But this doesn't usually happen, and if you've got someone waiting for you at home, it's up to you not to *let* it happen. If your relationship is solid and you value it, you should be able to live your passions for both tango and your non-dancing loved one to the fullest.

Whatever your partner situation, you're dancing tango to have fun and to add something positive to your life. To continue to do both these things, remember:

- To seek solutions, not blame.
- To laugh off mistakes.
- That tango is about what happens on the dance floor, not beyond.

In the end, relationship issues might make you decide that tango is not for you. You might even blame tango for seemingly new issues that have come up in your relationship. Or you might use tango to work through some of your issues—and your relationship will be stronger for it.

~ Lesson 23 ~

TANGO IS A VOYAGE OF SELF-DISCOVERY

Studying dance is as much about developing awareness as developing specific skills. Just as we learn a lot about others through the way they dance, we can also learn a lot about ourselves.

Body awareness is the ability to understand how our bodies move and where they are in space. Physical disciplines such as dance both require and improve our proprioception, which is the sense that allows us to control our body parts without looking at them.

Self-awareness is having a clear perception of our personality, including strengths, weaknesses, thoughts, beliefs, motivations, and emotions, then taking control of these aspects of ourselves. Tango can help us build this understanding as well.

So to improve in tango, we need to know not only our physical strengths, weaknesses, and tendencies but also our psychoemotional ones: Am I receptive? Reactive? Defensive? Controlling? Passive? Impatient? Is it easy for me to assert myself? To let go?

Here are a few things I've learned or confirmed about myself over the years, with a little help from tango.

I enjoy intensity. I'm certain this is one of the principal qualities that attracts me to tango. Not a lukewarm kind of person, I enjoy rich food, strong coffee, robust wine, scary movies, loud music, hot showers, and demanding workouts. I also like intense human connections: While I'm not big on small talk, I love deep conversation—or a profoundly connected *tanda*. Tango dancers are such an eclectic bunch that I've often wondered if one of the common threads that weave us together is a desire for intense sensations or connections.

Tango allows me to let go. This is one of the other main attractions of the dance for me. Stillness of mind doesn't come easy. I'm a busy person, and my busy brain can keep me awake at night for hours. I worry and I stress—until I hit the dance floor, where the music, movement, and human contact all combine to create my great escape. Out on the floor, in the arms of a dancer, to the beat of a beautiful soundtrack . . . Everything disappears but the here and now. It's not only completely enjoyable; it is also tremendously therapeutic.

I go with the flow. I've always loved surprises, and I'm quite capable of taking the situation I'm given and running with it. I roll with the punches, so to speak. This makes me a natural follower: I don't overthink what's happening and I'm pretty good at accepting what comes, no matter how unexpected it is. I think this also makes me a patient leader: I'm not overly attached to the past or the previous plan.

I may be a patient leader, but I'm also a confident one. It did take me time to build that confidence, though. As I mentioned in Lesson 15, it's important to have clear intentions in life and in tango. Know what you want, say what you want, go after what you want. None of these are skills that come naturally to me, but tango and teaching have helped me develop them. I certainly went after what I wanted when my partner and I opened our school, MonTango, more than a dozen years ago. It has since grown into one of our city's main tango spots. This has taught me that dreams are worth pursuing.

I don't always fit in. I think this is one of the reasons I like to be the host, the teacher, the DJ. If I'm just another participant, I sometimes feel like a bit of a misfit. And I've always felt this way: Throughout school and in my previous career, I was never part of the "in" crowd or the cool clique. I never knew how to pretend to be just like everybody else, how to act a certain way or say the "right" things to get in with the "right" people. Don't get me wrong—while I was a bit of an outsider, I was never an outcast. I had a small group of very close friends and always got along with most people. It's just that I didn't often have that sense of belonging. Sometimes I wonder if this isn't another common thread in tango. This milieu is so full of odd (and wonderful) characters that it sometimes feels like a reunion of misfits. Then again, there *are* cliques in tango. I'm just not a part of them and they don't thrive at my *milongas*. I think what I've figured out is that in tango, as in life, I always prefer inclusivity to exclusivity.

My limits exist to be pushed. Sometimes I think I would like to live a simpler, quieter life. But every time I go for something simple, I end up taking it further than intended. This has been evident in my tango journey: Not content to just dance, I began to teach; not content to just teach, I opened my own school; not content with teaching and running a school, I also perform and produce shows, DJ, blog . . . And, of course, I have continued my own dance, movement, and teacher training, taking privates whenever possible, learning to lead, and getting certified as a fitness instructor and a yoga instructor. I don't know what my next big step will be, but I know once I get comfortable where I am, I won't stay there for long.

I will never believe I am enough. I think the continued desire to learn, advance, and grow is a good thing, but in my case it's also a sign that I never feel I do enough—or that I'm good enough at anything I do. For example, I will never be the dancer I want to be. This is both a good and a bad thing. It means I get very down on myself at times, especially after watching myself perform. But it also means I push myself harder every time and therefore—I can admit it—I improve.

I love teaching. I may not feel I've become the dancer I strive to be, but I do know that I'm a good teacher. It's because I'm as passionate about teaching as I am about dancing. Looking back, I think I'm twice (or more) the teacher now that I was when I started out, and I plan to continue my growth. All the lessons

I've mentioned here—and more—have taught me how to better teach others.

So what have you learned through tango? Has it helped you grow and evolve as a person as well as a dancer? Has it opened your eyes to something you didn't know about yourself?

~ Lesson 24 ~

MEDITANGO: A BENEFICIAL
PRACTICE

Lots of people say that tango is a form of meditation. I even
say it myself. But is it really?

I know more about meditation than I once did, and while I'm not so sure this dance can be considered actual meditation, I do believe it shares many of the same qualities and benefits.

Meditation has been proven to reduce stress and anxiety. Study after study has shown this. And we know that physical activities such as dancing also offer great benefits in this area. But guess what? Tango in particular is a well-documented stress and anxiety reducer. (I even once gave a presentation on tango for stress reduction to a group of educators.)

Meditation improves concentration. The practice of mindfulness meditation begins with concentration exercises, which may eventually lead to a meditative state. In the practice of yoga, there are eight limbs, or steps. The physical poses (asanas) are third, while concentration (sixth) comes before meditation (seventh). Tango, too, is an exercise in focus and concentration. We have various tools (music, movement, a partner) at our disposal to help us. Many meditation techniques also use tools (a guiding voice, a chant, our own breath) to aid focus.

Meditation has been shown to increase happiness. This ultimately improves practitioners' self-image and outlook on life. If you dance tango, I don't need to tell you that it, too, can bring new joy to your life. The socialization aspect, the enjoyment of the music, and the sense of accomplishment as we improve our skills are all proven mood-boosters.

Both meditation and tango increase self-awareness. As we learn tango, we develop an awareness of our bodies that in turn develops our overall self-awareness.

The two practices have been shown to slow the aging process. Meditation can reduce age-related memory loss, while tango is increasingly used as a therapy for people with such diseases as Parkinson's and Alzheimer's. Partner dancing improves the ability to multi-task—for example, navigating in space while remaining in sync with your partner. Research has shown that Argentine tango offers particular benefits for the brain, probably due to its improvised nature.

On a psycho-emotional level, meditation and tango have much in common. Being a good tango dancer and attentive partner involves some letting go of the ego, which is an important concept in meditation. Tango dancers also need to be able to let go of the plan—another meditation concept. And have you ever taken a tango class in which the teachers didn't mention the need to be present? In the moment, in your body, for your partner. Meditation, too, is an exercise in presence.

Anecdotally, people who compare tango to meditation all say the same thing: It allows us to let go of our thoughts, worries, and stresses and to live completely in the moment. This is one of the things that drew me to dance and to Argentine tango. As I mentioned, I have an overly busy brain—the kind that loves to wake me up at 3 a.m. or to distract me from the task at hand—and tango is one of the only activities that is pretty much guaranteed to still my mind and make me fully, truly present. Meditation attracts me for the same reasons, though the work is more challenging for me without the music, movement, and human contact to help.

I can't write about meditation and tango without mentioning yoga. Yoga is not a synonym for meditation—you can do the physical part of yoga without practising meditation and you can practise meditation without yoga. But in my personal experience as a yoga practitioner and teacher, the two are inseparable. Real yoga is much more than downward dog and sun salutations, and meditation is an integral part of it. If we add the benefits of the yoga poses to those of the meditative process, the similarities with tango only multiply. Both yoga and tango improve our posture, alignment, strength, mobility, balance, and cardiovascular health. In yoga, the physical poses come before meditation because if we are not able to be well aligned and well positioned, we will be uncomfortable and have difficulty meditating. In tango, if we are not well aligned and well positioned, we will have difficulty dancing because we and our partners will be uncomfortable.

My partner once said to me, "What yoga is to fitness, tango is to dance." Yoga and tango both require an awareness of body and self that is not as present, or at least not often taught, in many other forms of exercise or social dance.

Even the advice I read about learning meditation resembles that which I give my tango students. Here are some examples of the similarities:

- Consistent practice matters more than long practice. Better a few short sessions a week than just one long one.
- If your mind wanders, that's okay and maybe even a good thing. In meditation, we want to notice what's happening in our minds and redirect our thoughts back to the focus of our practice. If your mind wanders, it doesn't mean you are not meditating. And if your mind wanders while you're dancing, it means you're not overthinking and you're dancing what you feel, using your instinct rather than your conscious mind.
- Avoid striving for perfection. Even long-time practitioners find meditation challenging. And even professional

maestros find tango challenging. Both are lifelong, life-enhancing practices that are about reaping the benefits of the journey rather than trying to reach a final destination.

So how is tango *not* like meditation?

Tango is a social activity, which is probably the biggest difference; meditation is a pretty solitary pursuit. However, meditation is centred around the connection to oneself, and we also have to connect to ourselves if we want to improve our dancing.

In tango, you are using tools—music and movement—that help channel your concentration and distract you from your busy mind and the outside world. My yoga teacher might argue that this is not true meditation, because distractions are, well, distracting us from the process. However, tango is certainly a type of concentration exercise, and concentration is a step on the path to meditation.

A few years ago, I went on a meditation retreat. Along with the many hours of silent, seated meditation, we practised what is called walking meditation. This exercise involved walking through the woods in silence, trying to be present and fully focused on our movements, surroundings, and sensations. Sounds a lot like tango, doesn't it? Minus the music and partner, of course.

So I guess tango, while not medit*ation*, could at the very least be called medit*ative*. In any case, it benefits us in a lot of the same ways.

~ Lesson 25 ~

FOLLOWING YOUR PASSION IS SCARY, BUT WORTH IT

When I was a little girl, I wanted to be an actress, a dancer, and a writer. The path of my life has by no means been a straight one, and what I thought those things would mean was quite different from what they turned out to be. But almost half a century later, I realize that the job I have now means I get to be all those things and more.

Through my tango school, I wear the hats of dancer, teacher, studio owner, event organizer, performer, show producer, DJ, and (now) writer. All this means I work pretty hard most of the time, but since I love what I do, it often doesn't actually feel that much like work.

The tango business is not always easy, but I count myself lucky to do what I do, because my days are filled with these activities:

Dancing. As I said, I always wanted to be a dancer. I took my first ballet class at four years old, and while I gave up the ballerina dream—and, in my teenage years, ballet altogether—I have not stopped dancing since. The fact that I get to dance every day keeps me happy and healthy, body and soul.

Teaching. I grew up with an intense fear of public speaking, and in my youth I never, ever imagined I would become a teacher. But I began teaching through my previous career in journalism. I was the main newsroom trainer on new technologies at the newspaper I worked at, and for years I taught a university course on newspaper design. This was all terrifying to me at first, but I grew to love teaching—and people kept telling me I was good at it. Teaching is both challenging and rewarding, and I can truly say I'm passionate about it. Once I started teaching tango, well . . . I really knew I was on to something.

Connecting with people. Beyond the dance itself, this is what tango is all about. I love people, all kinds of people, and tango is full of human connections that are varied, often intense, fascinating, and satisfying.

Building a community. My partner and I didn't necessarily plan this one when we were launching our little tango school, but we realized pretty early on that we were not just teaching people to dance—we were creating a community and therefore facilitating the forging of all kinds of relationships. I love seeing friendships and partnerships forming around me (partly thanks to me).

Throwing parties. Throughout my teens and 20s, I loved to throw parties. It was pretty straightforward to me: provide a table full of food, put on lots of loud dance music, and invite everyone I could think of. I loved planning the food, preparing the music, and building the guest list. So I guess it makes perfect sense that I enjoy hosting and DJing *milongas* every weekend.

Performing and producing shows. Had I started tango and plunged into it full time at a younger age, I would probably have done more of this. Despite my shyness, I do love to perform, and the experience of producing shows—with all the creativity and backstage excitement involved—is absolutely exhilarating.

DJing. This is another unexpected bonus of my job. From mix tapes to CDs to iTunes playlists, I have always loved putting music together. It doesn't matter whether it's for a workout, a car ride, or a party (though that last one's especially fun). These days, I can spend hours researching tango music—classic and alternative—and building *tandas* to play at *milongas*.

Working for myself. Again, not always easy, but so satisfying. It would be hard for me to go back to working for someone else at this point. It's not that I like being the boss so much (I don't think I'm very boss-like at all), but I sure like being the boss of *me*.

Working on myself. I've always been active. Tango helps me stay fit and mobile, and it makes me aware of my posture and the effect everything I do has on my partners. But it takes more than tango to keep in shape—for dance and for life. Besides my lifetime of dancing, I have run regularly for 30 years. (I keep trying to give it up because combined with all the tango it's too hard on my battered feet. But I just don't feel the same when I'm not getting that intense cardio!) Meanwhile, one of the most life-changing by-products of my tango career has been the discovery of yoga. I took it up a decade ago to try to increase my flexibility, but I quickly gained more than that: improved strength, better balance, and a whole new understanding of posture, alignment, and my own body and self. I have since delved ever deeper into yoga, exploring the aspects that go beyond the physical poses and obtaining several teaching certifications.

Writing. As I said, I always wanted to be a writer. English was my best and favourite subject through high school, and my post-secondary studies were all related to languages and literature. I studied translation for a while and worked as a copy editor for several years. I did some writing in that time but nothing regular. Several years ago, I realized that with all my observations and analytical thinking about tango, I should probably start writing things down. So I took the plunge and wrote my first blog post, and now I actually have a following! This year, I finally decided to compile some of my posts into this book, and I'm also working on the third draft of my first novel! (No, it's not about tango.)

Being a small-business owner is not always easy. And the tango business, because it is so close to my heart, can be tough emotionally as well as financially. But the rewards of doing what

I love make up for the fact that I work long, late hours and don't make much money.

When I was contemplating leaving my career as a copy editor to start a tango school, my mother and my financial advisor told me not to do it. I had young children, benefits, a pension plan, and debt; opening a small dance school as I was pushing 40 was not a sensible choice. But I couldn't ignore the tears I shed and the aching, empty pit I felt in my stomach once I had decided *not* to pursue what was probably my last opportunity to follow my lifelong dreams. So I did it. I had the full support of my partner and a year's worth of money to make a go of it. We held hands and we jumped, taking our young family with us.

This year, our tango school celebrates its 13th anniversary. It has been difficult and demanding at times (even before COVID-19), but I have never regretted the plunge I took a decade ago. I know with absolute certainty that had I not taken it, I would be regretting it every day.

And when I'm compiling *tandas* for an upcoming *milonga*, laughing with students as I help them execute a difficult move, or mingling with dancers at an event I'm hosting, I still can't get over how lucky I am to do what I do.

The lesson I leave you with is this: If you have a passion, follow it. And don't let fear hold you back.

~ Bonus Lesson ~

TANGO TERMINOLOGY

This is not meant to be a complete glossary of tango vocabulary. It contains most or all of the tango terms used in this book as well as some additional commonly used ones you might hear in the context of a lesson or a *milonga*.

Abrazo. Hug. The tango embrace or arm position and hold. Dancers can use an *abrazo abierto,* or open embrace, maintaining some distance between the upper bodies, or an *abrazo cerrado,* or close embrace, with contact between the partners' torsos. Close-embrace dancing is more difficult to master for most, but it also tends to be the preferred choice for high-level social dancers.

Adelante. Forward.

Adorno. Adornment, embellishment, or decoration. Footwork or flair added by either partner during *paradas* and pauses or between actions.

Apertura. Aperture or opening. Used to describe a *salida* to the side, specifically to the leader's left. See *Salida.*

Argentine tango. Synonymous with tango, which is the music and accompanying dance that originated more than a century ago in Río de la Plata; the port cities of Buenos Aires, Argentina; and Montevideo, Uruguay. We specify *Argentine* tango to differentiate it from the tango danced in ballroom dancing, which has been drastically transformed into something very stylized and showy and has been regulated for competition.

Arrastre. Drag. See *Barrida*.

Atrás. Backward.

Balanceo. Rock step. Useful for avoiding collisions, playing with rhythm, and making direction changes in small spaces. May also refer to a subtle shifting of weight from foot to foot in place and in time with the music at the beginning of a dance. Also called *cadencia*.

Baldosa. Tile. See *Cuadrado*.

Barrida. Sweep. One partner's foot makes contact with the other's foot and then moves it to a new position on the floor without losing contact. Also called *arrastre*, or drag.

Basic step. See *Paso básico*.

Boleo. Sometimes spelled *voleo*. A move where the free leg does a backward, forward, or wrapping projection or kick, usually in response to a change of energy or direction (most often a change of pivot). The word probably comes from *boleadoras*, a type of throwing weapon made of weights on the ends of cords. This weapon was once used by *gauchos* to capture animals by entangling their legs, and it is now used as a percussive instrument in a type of Argentine folkloric dance. Some argue that *voleo* is the correct spelling, deriving from the word *volear,* which means to throw or "volley," as with a ball. Note that it is never spelled (or pronounced) *bolero,* which can refer either to an entirely different genre of Latin music and dance or to a short jacket modelled after those worn by Spanish bullfighters.

Cabeceo. Nod. From the word *cabeza,* meaning head. It refers to the traditional, non-verbal look-and-nod technique for selecting dance partners from a distance in *milongas.* Also see *Mirada.*

Cadencia. See *Balanceo.*

Calesita. Carousel. A figure in which the leader walks around his partner while keeping her pivoting on her supporting leg.

Caminata. Walk. Generally considered the true basic step of Argentine tango. Great dancers are appreciated for the quality of their tango walk above all. The tango walk should have a feline quality, at once powerful and smooth, emphasizing both the grounding and propulsion of the supporting leg and the extension of the free leg.

Candombe. A type of dance originally danced by the descendants of black enslaved people in the Río de la Plata region and still performed in Montevideo, Uruguay. The music is of African origin with a marked rhythm played on a kind of drum called a tamboril. It survives today as a rhythmic background to certain *milongas.*

Canyengue. An old style of tango from the very beginning of the 20th century. The music from this period had a faster or peppier 2/4 tempo, so the dance had a rhythmic flavour similar to that of modern *milonga*. A very close embrace was used as well as some unique posture, embrace, and footwork elements.

Colgada. Literally, it means hanging or dangling. In tango, it is a type of off-axis movement in a "V" position, where the couple's feet stay close and the upper bodies move away. The balance of the two dancers is based on counterweight, which they exert together in opposing directions.

Compás. The beat, or pulse, as in that of the music or that of your heart.

Cortina. Literally, it means curtain, but it describes the 30- to 60-second clip of non-tango music used to break up musical *tandas*, or sets.

Cruce. Cross. Refers to the basic crossed position, used most often by the follower, in which the left leg crosses in front of the right. Not to be confused with cross system.

Cuadrado. Square or box step. Sometimes called *baldosa,* or tile. A basic six-count sequence made up of forward, backward, and side steps.

Disociación. Dissociation. In tango, it refers to the very common situation in which the lower body and upper body don't face the same direction. This allows for freedom of movement with the legs while staying connected with the upper bodies. Dissociation can be achieved by keeping the chest position fixed (usually facing the partner) and turning the hips, or by keeping the hips fixed and turning the torso (usually toward the partner).

Enganche. Any leg-around-leg hooking action. Similar to and often interchangeable with *gancho*. Also see *Gancho*.

Enrosque. Screw. An *adorno* in which one pivots in place while the feet are crossed. Often done by skilled leaders during *giros*.

Follower. The partner dancing what was traditionally the woman's role. In the interest of inclusiveness and reflecting reality, there has been a general movement to stop using the terms "man" and "woman" altogether within the context of tango-dancing roles and to always use the gender-neutral "leader" and "follower." The problem is these limited words are pretty faulty descriptions of what the two roles are all about. They make it sound like the leader is the dominant partner and the follower is passive, even submissive. The terms really do not describe what truly happens between the two partners. The much more complex process goes something like this: The "leader" invites the "follower" to execute a movement; the "follower" executes the movement she felt; the "leader" follows his partner through the completion of that movement (whether or not it was the movement he intended); and the whole process starts again. An experienced follower can even influence the leader's choices by adding *adornos* and her own musical interpretation. Some go so far as to argue that the follower is in fact the real leader, because regardless of the leader's original intention, he (or she or they) has to follow through on his partner's actual interpretation and execution of the lead. Also see *Leader*.

Gancho. Hook. A move wherein you hook or catch your partner's leg with your own. Note that it's a *gancho* and not a *gaucho*. A *gaucho* is an Argentinian cowboy.

Giro. Turn. One partner, usually the leader, turns more or less on the spot while the follower does a *molinete,* or grapevine, sequence around him. Also see *Molinete.*

Lápiz. Pencil. Circular embellishments "drawn" on the floor by either partner.

Leader. The partner dancing what was traditionally the man's role. There has been a general movement to stop using the terms "man" and "woman" altogether within the context of tango-dancing roles and to always use the gender-neutral "leader" and "follower." Interestingly, the terms "leader" and "follower" are not really used in Spanish. When referring to the partners, Spanish-speaking teachers often stick to *hombre* (man) and *mujer* (woman), which, while not gender-neutral, don't restrict the partners to one active and one passive role. When referring to the action of the man, or leader, they say *marcar,* which means to mark or indicate, not lead. The woman, or follower, *acompaña* (accompanies) or *se deja llevar* (lets herself be led). These terms have a less passive connotation and imply that it is her choice. Remember that at the beginning of the 20th century, when there were many more men than women in Argentina, men learned tango together, practising and mastering both roles before having the privilege of dancing with a woman. Also see *Follower.*

Marca. Mark. The lead.

Milonga. Because this word has a triple meaning, it can be confusing for novices.

1. One of the three musical genres that make up Argentine tango: tango, *milonga,* and *vals* (waltz). *Milonga* music is in

2/4 time. (Tango music can be in 2/4 or 4/4 and *vals* is in 3/4.) *Milonga* has a very rhythmic, strongly accented beat; it often contains an underlying *habanera* rhythm and is generally faster and more joyful than tango music. It has its own dancing style to go with it: Dancers avoid pausing, mostly stay in parallel system, and often use double-time steps, referred to as *milonga traspié*. *Milonga* dancing uses the same basic elements as tango, with a strong emphasis on the rhythm. Figures tend to be less complex than many of those used in tango.

2. The name given to any venue dedicated to Argentine tango (usually a dance school that also holds such dancing events as *prácticas* and *milongas*).

3. The name given to Argentine tango social-dancing events.

So you get all dressed up to go dancing at a *milonga,* where you will hear and dance to *milonga.*

Milonguero/Milonguera. A dancer who frequents *milongas* (as opposed to a stage dancer, for example). Generally, this label is reserved for dancers of a certain level. *Milonguero* can also refer to an old style of tango dancing wherein the couple held such a close embrace that the follower couldn't really turn her hips. This style gave birth to figures in which pivoted *ochos* are re-placed by crosses, such as the *ocho cortado* and *ocho milonguero.*

Mirada. Look. Paired with the *cabeceo,* it completes the tradi-tional look-and-nod system for selecting dance partners in the *milonga.* Also see *Cabeceo.*

Molinete. Literally, it means windmill, but in dance it translates as grapevine. Made of the step sequence forward-side-back-ward-side (or sometimes forward-together-backward-together), it is most often danced in a circle by the follower around the leader to make a *giro*. Also see *Giro*.

Ocho. Eight or figure eight. A combination of pivots with either forward or back steps, which, when done in pairs, draws a figure eight shape on the floor. There are several variations of *ochos*:

- **Ocho adelante.** Forward figure eight.
- **Ocho atrás.** Backward figure eight.
- **Ocho cortado.** Cut figure eight. The forward pivot is interrupted to produce an abrupt sideways rock step followed by a direct return to the cross.

Parada. Stop. The leader halts the follower's action, simultaneously placing his foot against hers. Often used in combinations with the sandwich. Also see *Sandwich*.

Paso básico. Basic step. While the real basic step in Argentine tango is generally considered to be the walk, this eight-count structure has been used as a basic teaching sequence for decades. It is a remarkably controversial little sequence. Still used by many instructors, it is shunned by others. Supporters believe it's a useful pedagogical tool that contains essential elements such as forward, back, and side steps as well as the cross. Detractors say it's pointless to teach a "basic step," arguing that dancers will either not use it in real-life social dancing or will become dependent on it, thus never learning to improvise properly.

Planeo. Literally, it means glide. Similar to a *calesita*, the *planeo* involves one partner walking around the other, pivoting him or her on the supporting leg, but in a *planeo*, the free leg is extended so that it "draws" an arc on the floor.

Práctica. Practice. A tango-dancing event that is much less formal than a *milonga*. Floorcraft and following the *ronda* are generally less strictly adhered to or enforced during *prácticas*, so dancers can work on their moves and technique. Talking while dancing is also tolerated. It is usually suggested that tango students attend *prácticas* for a while before moving on to *milongas*. During a *práctica*, teachers may or may not be present and may or may not lead the practice by suggesting or teaching exercises or figures.

Rebote. Rebound. A rock step wherein the dancers rewind a step by pushing against the floor to go back to the previous position.

Ronda. Literally, it means round. In tango, it is what we usually call the "line of dance" in English. The *ronda* in tango always circulates in a counter-clockwise direction around the dance floor. Couples are expected to follow the general flow of the dancers ahead of them, resisting the urge to cut ahead of slower-moving dancers or to stay in one spot blocking traffic. On larger dance floors, there can be several *rondas* at a time: one at the outer edge of the floor, generally reserved for more experienced and disciplined dancers, and up to three more smaller *rondas* inside, like lanes on a racetrack. It is bad form to zigzag haphazardly from one *ronda* to the next; lane changes should be made sparingly and with caution.

Sacada. From the verb *sacar*, which means to remove. In tango, one partner steps right into his or her partner's space, seemingly forcing the partner to switch places and sometimes provoking an embellishment by the other person if there was contact with the recipient's free leg.

Salida. Literally, it means exit, but it actually refers to the opening step of a dance or a sequence.

Sandwich. Also referred to as the *sanguche, sanguchito,* or *mordida* (bite). During a *parada,* one partner sandwiches the other's foot between his or her own. See *Parada.*

Sistema cruzado. Cross system. Refers to the walking relationship between the two partners. In cross system, the two partners are stepping with the same leg: left to left or right to right. At least 50 percent of figures use the cross system. *Ochos,* for example, most often take place in cross system. Also see *Sistema paralelo.*

Sistema paralelo. Parallel system. Refers to the walking relationship between the two partners. In parallel system, which is basically just the normal walking system, the leader walks in line with his partner. The partners walk in step with each other, but they are on opposite legs: leader's left to follower's right or vice versa. In parallel system, each partner is the mirror image of the other. Also see *Sistema cruzado.*

Tanda. A set of songs for dancing. Generally, *tandas* are three or four songs long. (They used to sometimes be as long as five, but that is rare these days.) They will be of one genre (tango, *milonga,* or *vals*) and are most often all by the same orchestra and from the same decade (or even the same year), perhaps even with the same singer. *Tandas* can also be compiled of songs by different orchestras with a similar sound and feel. In a *milonga,* the format is generally as follows: two *tandas* of tango, one *tanda* of *vals,* two *tandas* of tango, one *tanda* of *milonga,* and repeat.

Tango. The music and accompanying dance that originated in Río de la Plata more than a century ago. Also see *Argentine tango.*

Tanguero/tanguera. A tango dancer. *Tanguero* for a man, *tanguera* for a woman.

Vals. One of the three musical genres that make up Argentine tango: tango, *milonga,* and *vals* (waltz). *Vals* music is played in 3/4 time. (*Milonga* is in 2/4, while tango music can be in 2/4 or 4/4.) Dancers use the same steps and technique in *vals* as in tango, but they tend to select quicker, more rhythmic figures that flow, rock, and turn in order to express both the feeling and rhythmic structure of the music. They use the first beat in the measure as their basic walking beat, adding accelerated steps or *adornos* on the second and/or third beats as they wish.

Volcada. Literally, it means overturned or tipped over. In tango, it is an off-axis move in which the follower leans forward, supported by the leader's torso or arms. Usually, the forward "fall" is accompanied by a sweeping *adorno* of the follower's free leg.

Voleo. See *Boleo.*

Andrea Shepherd
Photo by Isabelle-Blanche Pinpin

ABOUT THE AUTHOR

Born in Toronto and raised in Montreal, Andrea Shepherd has written and danced all her life. She took her first ballet class at age 4, dabbled in everything from tap dancing to theatre to salsa, and finally fell head-over-stiletto-heels in love with Argentine tango in her late 20s.

In school, English was always Andrea's best and favourite subject, though she was never much of a student. She started keeping a diary at age 10 and wrote just about every day for 20 years. She started writing her first novel at age 13 and finally completed one at age 51.

In 1989, Andrea got a clerical job in the newsroom at the Montreal Gazette. She remained there for 19 years, working her way up to a copy-editing position and writing the occasional feature article. Andrea also taught a desktop publishing course in Concordia University's Journalism Department for a decade. In 2008, she left her career to pursue dance full time. Against all odds and sensible advice, she and her partner opened a tango studio, which has become one of the top Argentine tango schools in Montreal.

In 2014, Andrea partnered up her love of dance and writing when she created the blog *Life Is a Tango*. It gained more of a following than she ever expected and eventually became this book.

Andrea lives in Montreal with her partner, Wolf, son, Shane, and daughter, Mia.

Made in the USA
Monee, IL
18 June 2021

71213793R10095